Bob Fisher and Barry Pickthall

Ocean Conquest

In July 1972, Whitbread announced it would sponsor the first fully-crewed yacht race around the world. This was a courageous decision, as no one knew what the outcome would be. Since that first successful Whitbread in 1973-74, Whitbread has been proud to have been involved in the development of the world's premier ocean race.

In its 250-year history, Whitbread has always been involved in the community. Even now, as one of the leading drinks, food and leisure companies in the UK, Whitbread is continuing to 'put something back' through sports and its broadly-based community investment programme.

The Whitbread Round The World Race brings out the best in people – even to participate, let alone win – the competitors need courage, endurance, efficiency, self-reliance, leadership and teamwork. These qualities are just as important in the business world and the competitors are an inspiration to Whitbread and to all companies involved in the race.

In September 1993, a new generation of boats and crews will leave Southampton to embark on the sixth Whitbread Round The World Race. As always the competitors will have stretched the boundaries of technology and innovation to produce the fastest yachts possible under the rules, and the sailors will be the best ocean yachtsmen in the world. This is possible because of the efforts of those involved in the five previous races. The continuity of the Whitbread Round The World Race is a tribute to all those who have experienced the excitement, endured the dangers and discomforts and found personal satisfaction and achievement.

For the 1993-94 Race, Whitbread has been joined by Heineken, the Dutch beer company, and BT, Britain's leading telecommunications company. Heineken has been a business partner of Whitbread's since 1961, and will present the overall winner in each class with the Heineken Trophy. A trophy for the winner of each leg will also be presented. BT, which has been involved since the fourth race, has developed new technology which will contribute greatly to the media coverage of the event. This book is a celebration of what has been achieved so far and an indication of what will be achieved in 1993.

The principal reason for Whitbread PLC's longevity and success is the company's forward-thinking and dynamic outlook. The company continues to strive to be the best in all its fields of endeavour. The Whitbread Round The World Race is a highly visible symbol of that philosophy.

Martin Findlay
Chairman of the Race Board 1993

BARIENT

Bob Fisher and Barry Pickthall

Ocean Conquest

LITTLE BROWN AND COMPANY
BOSTON · TORONTO · LONDON

A LITTLE, BROWN BOOK

DESIGNED BY GARY OTTEWILL
TECHNICAL EDITOR ADRIAN MORGAN

THE PUBLISHERS WISH TO THANK
JENNIE FITZHARDINGE, PRESS OFFICER FOR THE WHITBREAD ROUND THE WORLD RACE,
FOR HER HELP IN COMPILING CHAPTER TEN: THE 1993-4 ENTRANTS

ISBN 0-316-90469-4
A CIP CATALOGUE RECORD FOR THIS BOOK
IS AVAILABLE FROM THE BRITISH LIBRARY.

TYPESET BY SX COMPOSING, ESSEX
COLOUR SEPARATIONS BY FOTOGRAPHICS, HONG KONG
PRINTED IN ENGLAND BY BUTLER & TANNER, SOMERSET

LITTLE, BROWN AND COMPANY (UK) LTD
165 GREAT DOVER STREET, LONDON SE1 4YA

Contents

Ocean Conquest

Part One: The Previous Races

Part Two: The Last Race

Part Three: The 1993 · 94 Race

Part Four: Results and Index

Foreword

Peter Blake OBE

The only competitor to have raced in all previous Whitbreads

Picture the scene in your mind. It's very cold; even down below the temperature is only just above freezing. Large drops of condensation are running back and forth across the deckhead just above your face in time to the roll of the yacht. Your sleeping bag and pillow are damp and have been like that for two weeks now. You are wearing all of your clothes in your bunk to try and get some warmth into your body after four hours on watch in atrocious conditions. Your feet are still cold, although a tingling feeling in your toes announces the return of circulation which had stopped after standing in the slushy snow that has built up in the corners of the cockpit. The noise of the sea running past the hull is like an express train that never stops, and this is accompanied by the ceaseless racket of the spinnaker sheet being eased and then ground back in again on the winch drum mounted right overhead.

The sea is still very rough from the never-ending march of gales that hit as your yacht dropped through the Roaring Forties into the Howling Fifties. Only your Sony Walkman headphones and some loud music have allowed you to catch any sort of sleep at all. In the last few days you have listened to *Aspects of Love* and *Phantom of the Opera* so many times just to drown out the sailing noises that you need to forget for a few brief moments.

The cook is rattling the pans in the galley – breakfast is not far away. And you can hear the sound of hail hammering on the deck in a passing squall. It's time to get up and get ready for the next four hours. But it's very hard to move. Just five minutes more; you are feeling almost warm for the first time.

But breakfast is ready and it's time to go. So, down with the leecloth, out of the sleeping bag and over the edge to drop onto the bunk below – the floor is covered in soggy sails, so better not stand there. Where are your boots that you put carefully in the passageway a few hours ago? But there have been a number of sail changes since then so you have to hunt for them.

And you need a pee. Urgently. But someone else is already 'in there' with others waiting. You ask 'whoever is in there' to pass out a plastic bag. There is very little privacy in anything you do. With your wet-weather trousers on, (soggy), you make your way to the galley for a bowl of porridge, covered with brown sugar and reconstituted powdered milk. Then maybe a pancake or boiled egg or, even better, last night's freeze-dried leftovers that have been heated up. And, of course, the first of the never-ending mugs of sweet tea.

But you have forgotten to tape the foil over your feet, so it's off with the boots, wrap your feet in strips of 'space blanket' (which is, by the way, extremely effective), then back on with your socks and boots. Wet-weather jacket (wet), harness line, neck towel (soggy), balaclava, and Musto hat with the ear flaps (a must). Thermal mittens on, and a pair of full-leather sailing gloves in your pocket and you are ready to go.

You slide back the hatch and it's like entering another world. Huge breaking seas come marching up from behind, with the tops of the crests blown away by the wind. It's bitterly cold – probably around minus five degrees centigrade, although last night the B&G read minus ten degrees. The watch on deck look worn out but with that glint in their eyes that tells you they are pleased it is you and not they who are going to be doing the racing for the next few hours.

The watch captain explains the situation: 'a small spinnaker, two reefs in the main, two in the mizzen but there has been no chance of a mizzen staysail for a couple of hours. There is a hole developing in the mainsail where it has been rubbing overnight on the upper spreader which will need something done about it fairly soon. We've seen three large 'bergs since dawn and more on the radar. More worryingly, with the sea temperature at minus two, the growlers and "bergy bits" aren't melting, and there have been a couple of close misses. So, keep a good look-out. We've done sixty miles in the last four hours, so try and beat that'. And 'See you later, we're off the bed. Have fun. Ha! Ha!'

The hatch slams and you and your watch are 'it' once again. And it's blowing very hard. With black snow squalls coming in from behind. And the yacht is on the verge of being out of control. It's both steering wheels all the time now, with the leeward man riding 'shotgun'. The spray coming over the windward deck is turning to ice particles. The decks are covered in ice. The coils of ropes in the bottoms of the cockpits are full of snow. And it's so bitterly cold. And this is supposed to be fun.

The hardships onboard a Whitbread yacht in the Southern Ocean are very real. And they don't go away. At times you are frightened by the sheer isolation, at times elated at seeing nature in a form that most will never believe possible. It's the experience of a lifetime. It's one you get to hate, but learn to love at the same time. Its been a major part of my life that I will never forget, or regret.

Peter Blake

***Steinlager 2*, Peter Blake's all-conquering ketch**
Her record in the 1989/90 race may never be equalled; winning all six legs is a feat which cannot be bettered.

Steinlager

Introduction

The Everest of Ocean Racing

The Whitbread Round The World Race has been called the Everest of ocean racing. A 33,000-mile race across the world's toughest oceans which pits crews as much against the elements as against their rivals. What began as an adventure has developed into a classic marathon which tests every crewman – and woman – to the limits of his or her ability. Crews preparing for the sixth running of the event which starts from Southampton in 1993, face storm-force winds, the threat of collision with icebergs, whales and an increasing amount of flotsam which broke bows and damaged keels and rudders during the last highly-publicized race in 1989/90. And if that were not enough, to keep their interest primed, there is the little matter of rounding Cape Horn where the winds are gale force most days, a storm the rest, building to hurricane force on an average of twelve days a year.

The first 6,300-mile stage of the race to the Uruguayan playground resort of Punta del Este, may represent a fair-weather 'trade wind cruise', but the nail-biting competition between two groups of maxi-yachts and sixty-footers will provide as big a test of nerves and temperament as boat speed. But it is over the next three legs down through the Roaring Forties to the Screaming Sixty latitudes that most crews sign up for. It is on the route to Fremantle, Australia and Cape Horn via Auckland, New Zealand where the race develops into a roller-coaster ride; where the difference between windswept and wipe-out is so often balanced on a knife edge.

Those who experience these wild winds for the first time yelp, partially in fear but principally for joy, the first time their yacht is picked up on the crest of a wave and surfs away in a plume of spray, touching thirty knots plus. The novelty never wears off.

Dutch skipper Cornelis van Rietschoten, whose two yachts, both named *Flyer*, won the 1977/78 and 1981/82 Whitbread races, describes it as one of the greatest sensations in life. 'It is as if a giant hand suddenly thrusts you forward. The yacht starts to hum like an electric train, vibrating from stem to stern. The bow wave grows higher and higher until all noise is drowned by the rushing water and spray. It's like riding a roller-coaster down a vertical track. You just hold your breath and hang on.'

Rear Admiral Otto Steiner, race chairman of the first two Whitbreads. Opposite: *The Card*.

The greatest danger is of broaching. A momentary lapse of concentration on the part of the helmsman or sail-trimmers and their charge will spin round out of control, flattened by the wind and at the mercy of the next foaming wave crest. Half an hour of wrestling with such danger is all that most helmsmen can stand.

Add to this the ever-present danger of losing a man overboard into these freezing waters, or crashing into hidden 'growlers' – semi-submerged breaks of ice from much larger icebergs – and it is understandable why this race is so often compared with climbing Everest.

The Whitbread, like the course, has grown in stature since the first 'cruise in company' back in 1973. The exploits of solo yachtsmen such as Francis Chichester, Alec Rose, Robin Knox-Johnston and Chay Blyth had all helped to awaken public awareness to the adventure of sailing around the world.

The idea of a fully-crewed race was first floated by Anthony Churchill and Guy Pearse. Their brochure, circulated during Cowes Week in August 1971, was well received among yachtsmen, but failed to attract the commercial sponsorship necessary to run the show. When the Royal Naval Sailing Association, RNSA, decided to pick up the gauntlet a year later, Pearse and Churchill, who had collected seventeen potential entries, handed over their files, and the Whitbread Brewery, which had already supported Chichester's earlier circumnavigation, agreed to back the venture.

The race has cost four lives, but those tragedies led to more stringent safety requirements for the second race in 1977/78 and a total review of equipment, construction and rescue techniques for the next event in 1993/94. The deaths have also done nothing to dampen the enthusiasm we all hold for escaping life's ruts. Indeed, from the early beginnings which saw fourteen of the original seventeen starters complete this formidable course, more than ninety crews had registered to compete in the sixth running of the event by December 1992, nine months before the start of the race.

The first Whitbread start, 8 September 1973; Chay Blyth and his paratroop crew win the start in *Great Britain II* from Frenchman Eric Tabarly in *Pen Duick VI*.

Part One

The Previous Races

Chapter One

The 1973·74 Race

On 8 September 1973, seventeen yachts from seven nations mustered off Southsea Castle overlooking the Solent to await the cannon fired by Sir Alec Rose that would send them off into the unknown.

Sir Alec was one of the few at that time to have completed a circumnavigation in a yacht and he knew just what an adventure it would turn out to be. But for most of those crews, a trans-ocean crossing was the limit of their experience. How would a modern racing yacht behave in the daunting storm-tossed seas of the Southern Ocean? How would they fare off Cape Horn? Would rigging and equipment withstand the strain of 27,000 miles at sea? Far too many questions remained unanswered.

Roddy Ainslie and the crew of *Second Life* in Sydney, resplendent in sponsored shirts – one of their few perks.

Favourite to win the first-ever Whitbread was Eric Tabarly, the French yachting hero who had already won two single-handed transatlantic races. He had also tamed the 605-mile Sydney/Hobart classic, and his 73ft alloy ketch *Pen Duick VI*, built specifically for the Whitbread race, epitomized the very latest thinking in ocean racing.

Against him was ranged the former British paratrooper Chay Blyth with a twelve-strong team of fellow 'Red Beret' fitness fanatics. Chay's plan to keep his crew on a curry diet throughout prompted many jokes but not about his new yacht – designed by Alan Gurney, modelled on the famous maxi *Windward Passage*. This 77ft ketch was funded by the Bahamian-based philanthropist 'Union' Jack Hayward and carried the name of Isambard Kingdom Brunel's first iron steamship, SS *Great Britain*, which Hayward paid to have salvaged from a beach on the Falklands and returned for restoration to her home port of Bristol.

Great Britain II was one of the first yachts to exploit early glassfibre-reinforced foam-sandwich construction techniques and, to the credit of her builder, went on to complete five further circumnavigations, including all the Whitbread races to date.

Not to be outdone, other divisions of Britain's armed forces entered yachts. The Army commandeered Chay Blyth's 59ft *British Steel* which had already completed one circumnavigation – against the prevailing wind and currents – and re-named her *British Soldier*. The Navy chose the 55ft Camper & Nicholson-designed *Adventure*, the first in a line of training yachts that continue to see service with the Joint Services Adventure Centre at HMS Hornet, a stone's-throw across Portsmouth Harbour from HMS Vernon which first hosted the fleet of Whitbread yachts.

Another potentially strong challenger was *Second Life*, the first production Ocean 71 yacht, skippered by Roddie Ainslie. He had rallied together twelve paying passengers, including Rob James, a man who was to later earn a unique place in the race's history.

Also from Britain was the hastily-built 80ft *Burton Cutter*, the largest yacht in the race. Paid for by Alan Smith, a wealthy West Country entrepreneur and sponsored to the tune of £10,000 (a great deal of money in those Corinthian days) by his tailor, the Whitbread was effectively *Burton Cutter*'s first trial sail.

Peter Blake, a twenty-five-year-old recruit from New Zealand who had signed on as watch-leader for the first of what was to be five Whitbread races, later recalled: 'We never had a chance to sail the boat before the start and were totally unprepared. As we set off down the Solent, we had a drum of rope in the cockpit and I was cutting off the sheets to size each time we hoisted a new sail.'

On board *Pen Duick VI*, Tabarly had recruited Marc Pajot, an Olympic silver-medallist, destined later to take on the great man's mantle. But other yachts flying the *tricouleur*, also appeared strong. There was André Viant with his 60ft staysail schooner, *Grand Louis*; two great long-distance men, Michel Malinovsky and Alain Gliksman aboard Jack Grout's 66ft ketch *Kriter* and Pierre Chassin's *Concorde*.

***Pen Duick VI*, Breton for 'little duck', Eric Tabarly's ketch with a spent uranium keel which became the subject of major controversy.**

Burton Cutter, the aluminium maxi-rater which Leslie Williams took to first place into Cape Town in 1973. On the next leg, she retired with serious hull damage.

From Italy came Giorgio Falck's 45ft wooden racing sloop *Guia*, *CS & RB*, a 50ft ketch skippered by Doi Malingri, and the 55ft yawl *Tauranga* sailed by Eric Pascoli.

Germany was represented by the 55ft traditional steel yawl *Peter von Danzig*, skippered by Reinhard Laucht. Poland boasted two yachts: *Copernicus*, a wooden 45ft ketch, entered by Olympic yachtsman Zygfryd Perlicki, and *Otago*, a 55ft steel ketch sailed by a crew of nine, led by Zdzislaw Pienkawa.

Mexico also had one representative – the washing machine millionaire Ramon Carlin, as yet unknown in the international sailing world. He had chosen the relative comfort of a Swan 65 production cruiser/racer, *Sayula II*, which escaped the notice of most pundits.

Joining the fleet for the first leg only was *Jakaranda*, John Goodwin's South African Admiral's Cup racer, and the Swedish yacht *Keewaydin* skippered by David Sundbaum which started a week late and never finished.

The course took the fleet first to Cape Town, then down through the Roaring Forties and Furious Fifties to Sydney, Australia in time for Christmas. On 29 December those who survived set out once more, this time bound for Cape Horn, before calling at Rio de Janeiro and returning to Portsmouth in April 1974. Just fourteen were to complete the distance.

First to run into trouble was the untried, hastily-built *Burton Cutter*, skippered by Les Williams, which had left the Solent with her crew still hammering their bunks together. There was also another problem which did not surface for two or three days. In their haste to finish the boat, someone forgot to connect the toilet piping to the outlet stopcock. 'Everything went straight into the bilge. The smell was dreadful!' Blake recalls, wrinkling his nose.

Later, the crew were forced to heave-to for a couple of days to cure the hull and deck leaks which showed up during the first gale. Despite these handicaps the course set by Williams, skirting the South Atlantic high-pressure system, well inside the traditional clipper route favoured by most others in the fleet, brought *Burton Cutter* into Cape Town first.

Over 2,200 miles away, Eric Tabarly suffered the nightmare of being dismasted, leaving him no option but to head *Pen Duick VI* towards Rio, 1,200 miles to the south east. Remarkably, a new spar was flown out in time for the French yacht to re-cross the Atlantic, arriving in Cape Town just two days before the re-start.

On handicap the Royal Navy's 55ft *Adventure*, skippered on the first leg by Patrick Bryans, which had finished a satisfying three hours ahead of the paratroopers on the larger *Great Britain II*, won the overall prize. The same yacht, but with a fresh crew, maintained this form on the second leg until rudder failure, deep in the Southern Ocean, robbed them of another stage victory – and almost certainly their claim to the Whitbread trophy.

This was the first time that modern yachts had ventured so far south and, for some, their worst fears were realised. *Great Britain II* lost her mizzen-mast; crewman Eddie Hope broke his arm. *Otago* lost the top third of her mizzen-mast and *Burton Cutter*'s crew was forced to make for Port Elizabeth after heavy pounding split the hull welding, flooding the forward watertight compartment. The yacht required such extensive repairs that the crew was forced to pull her out of the water and she did not re-join the race until the fleet arrived in Rio for the final leg home.

Tragically, two crew, Paul Waterhouse and Dominique Guillet were to lose their lives on this leg. Waterhouse, an army corporal, had sailed the first leg aboard *British Soldier* then changed yachts at Cape Town to sail the Southern Ocean leg aboard the Italian Swan 55 *Tauranga*. A genoa sheet whipped him off the

foredeck during a wild broach at night, in waters that are so cold no man can be expected to survive for more than twenty minutes. *Tauranga*'s crew suspect the blow was so strong that Waterhouse was unconscious when he hit the water, and they eventually gave up the search three hours later when worsening conditions threatened further casualties.

Three days later Dominique Guillet, co-skipper of the French yacht *33 Export*, was also swept off the bow by a wave while organising a headsail change. The force of water broke his lifeline and, after a fruitless thirty-minute search, his crew made the painful decision to save themselves and their boat, and headed despondently for Fremantle. Later, they rejoined the race, but not until two days after the fleet had left Sydney, bound for Cape Horn.

The toll might have been greater had luck not balanced out the effects of a freak wave that overwhelmed *Sayula II* during the same leg. She had been running before a 65-knot gale for two days and, judging from the angle of the kitchen knives that lodged themselves into the deckhead, the crew reckoned she had rolled through 170 degrees.

At 48 degrees 02 S, 90 degrees 37 E on 24 November *Sayula II* had capsized. Butch Dalrymple-Smith described what happened to the 65ft ketch and the way the crew restored the yacht they first believed was sinking.

'I was sitting in the dinette facing across the boat. I had just put a new tape in the eight-track – Led Zeppelin's *Houses of the Holy*. I can't hear that now without getting a little bit nervous. The boat

The Joint Services entry, *Adventure*, a mile from the finish of the second leg. She was to compete in two Whitbreads, placing third and seventh overall.

was sailing along smoothly and normally and then there was zero gravity – no up, no down. Then there was the most almighty crash and the side of the hull leapt towards me. I landed feet first on the cupboard which houses the eight-track, and fell in the corner between the deckhead and the cupboard.

An enormous pile of mattresses, floorboards and everything imaginable grew on the side of the saloon. And there was this regular, interminable rain of cans, water and bedding from the upper side; most of the tins bouncing off the deckhead on the way down to the pile. I did not feel upside down. It was rather like an hallucination. It is impossible to believe that your whole world has suddenly been turned upside down. But looking at all these things falling across the boat, you know that obviously something is amiss.

Keith Lorence was under the pile. How could he survive? I started heaving floorboards and stuff off him, but I think it all fell back down on him. Water was gushing in through a broken window in the cabin top. I followed him to the hatch, grabbing an oilskin jacket on the way. I felt the mast was bound to be over the side. 'Is it still up', I said, and it was. 'Let's get the sails off', he said.

We moved out on to the foredeck, slipping and sliding on salad oil and noodles that had mysteriously found their way on deck. We waited for help, fifteen seconds or so, and then, by ourselves, dropped the small staysail and tiny storm jib, the only sails we had been carrying. The two men on deck, Bob Martin and Roberto Cubas, had hauled themselves back on board the boat which was now on course again. We didn't realise at the time the difficulty they were having just physically turning the wheel because of all the broken gear, sheets and halyards draped across it.

The more immediate problems were inside the boat and we returned below. What a shambles there was. Ramon had already started bailing into the garbage bucket while someone else was pumping on the internal bilge pump. Ray was trying to transmit a PAN call, someone else was trying to get into the aft cabin. Another crewman was anxiously trying to hand the full garbage bucket out of the main hatch which was occupied by a party trying to get a crewman with a suspected broken leg below . . . All this in an area not much bigger than a telephone box.

Eventually, a semblance of order was restored. Cubas, the injured crewman, was laid out in the aft cabin and treated, two more bilge-pumps were brought into operation and a bucket chain got going. However, amidst this hive of activity, three or four of the crew, dazed and shocked, were meandering around vaguely, not knowing what to do. Bilge-water was pouring out from between the two starboard fuel tanks so I reckoned there must be a leak up there somewhere. And I was scared. We were about 49 degrees South, just over half way from Cape Town to Sydney with the water temperature 2 degrees centigrade. And I was sure we were sinking.

I thought the fuel tanks, which are very heavy, had punched a hole in the side of the hull when we fell off the wave because of all this water gushing down from underneath the fuel tanks. I realised much later that, when we tipped right over, we took in a lot of water which sat in the locker compartments up the side of the boat and it was this water rushing down, plus fresh water from two of the water tanks which broke their connections. We lost 140 gallons of fresh water this way. But after two hours of frantic effort, it became clear that we were not going to sink quite yet as we freed the bilge of most of its water. No bilge-pump worked more than half the time as there was so much muck in the bilge.

Clearing up, where do you start? The floorboards were all over the place. Chicken-noodle soup and salad oil everywhere made even standing hazardous. About five hours of back-breaking work followed and then, thanks to Yvonne, a hot supper. Cantis Orinday and Dave Bowen did the vital job of repairing the cabin window. The ship was safe and suddenly we began to feel cold. Then followed the coldest night in the world. The only four dry bunks were occupied by the wounded. All the mattresses in the main saloon were soaking. The six of us left to keep watch slept, or tried to sleep, in full oilskins on the bare floorboards. It was as cold and wet below as it was on deck.

The six exhausted watch-keepers spent two hours on and one hour off for the rest of the night. Although the wind was down to thirty knots, no one could work up enough enthusiasm to put up more than the No. 5 storm jib and storm staysail. That night we were in no mood to enjoy the most fantastic celestial light show in the southern sky: the southern Aurora in full blast. At first light, we had boiled eggs and then set the No. 3 jib poled out with full main in ten knots of wind from astern. Drying out began. With the deck looking like a Chinese laundry, we set the 1.5 oz spinnaker.

We knew it was all over at about 1100 (zone time) when Cantis and Ramon managed to start the engine on the first push of the button. Everything electrical and mechanical had been wiped dry and sprayed with WD40.

With the noise of the engine and the warmth of the sun, the wounded realised they were still alive and ventured forth. The six of us thankfully retired into the dry bunks, twenty-four hours after the capsize. Later, the opportunity came to compare experiences, to reflect, and piece together what really happened to *Sayula II* in the capsize.

The boat carried 400 gallons of fresh water in the standard tanks and about the same amount of diesel fuel. The hull itself is extremely strong and so are the masts. When Ramon suggested to Nautor they build an extra-strong mast they just laughed because they reckoned the mast was over-strong already. And they were right. The capsize came on the morning of 24 November at about 1000 local time. The timing was fortunate for it gave us a lot of daylight for recovering. The wind, north of west, had been blowing at fifty to fifty-five knots for two-and-a-half days. It did not give us any problems but it raised this appalling, unpredictable sea. I always visualized the Southern Ocean as endless lines of long rollers. It is not like that at all; the waves come at you in all directions. The waves are certainly big. I remember looking at one I believed was about as high as the boat is long.

But the ones to worry about are not the waves that look very

K
3138

K
356
K
3566
GREAT BRITAIN II

fierce as they roll down on you from astern, but the ones that start off small and suddenly peak absolutely underneath you. They don't necessarily come from astern, but often from the quarter. You cannot see this wave forming until a moment before it strikes the boat and then it is too late. It was this sort of wave that rolled *Sayula II*. Two men were on deck. Bob Martin, one of the best helmsmen we had, was steering and the other was Roberto Cubas. Both were clipped on. We had only a storm jib up, tiny sails, there mainly to make it easier for the helmsman to keep the head away.

Sayula II was on the face of the wave when the falling crest caught the stern first, forcing it down the wave faster than the bow. With the bow gripping the water and the stern in the falling water, the boat slewed around almost broadside on to the wave. And then the wave broke. The boat literally fell – no one knows how far. It was impossible to tell from below and the people on deck were up to their eyes in water so they could not see.

So the boat just dropped, and when it hit it was further over than horizontal because we broke the cabin window which meant we had hit partly on the deck. Everything fell out of its stowage. A peanut-butter jar broke on the main skylight. The tools in the workshop made nasty marks on the deckhead. From the trajectory these fallen articles must have taken, the angle was conservatively 155 degrees. In the after cabin, the marks caused by vodka bottles and other things that were stowed below the cabin sole would indicate the boat went over still further, to 170 degrees, which is near as dammit to upside down. But this may have been a slight distortion because of the flipping action of the stern as it fell. The Avon dinghy, which was stowed in one of the cockpit lockers, smashed through the seat above it and would have gone over the side had it not been caught by the mizzen boom. The broken Brookes and Gatehouse masthead unit and bent steaming light confirmed that the mast went well and truly under.

While both men in the cockpit were thrown off, both were hanging on to something belonging to the boat as well as being secured by their lifelines. Roberto was holding on to the stanchion down to leeward that was in fact dragging him under water. The mizzen boom dropped on his leg and he thought for a while it was broken. When he finally dragged himself back on board, the stainless-steel cliphook of his safety-harness was so badly distorted, it would not close. From then on, people on deck had at least two lifelines on and possibly more in similar circumstances.

Bob Martin was hanging on to the mizzen backstay and, when the boat recovered, was able to climb back aboard without much difficulty. So much water had flooded everywhere that there was not much difference in being on board and over the side. He was able to resume course before we dropped the sails.

While we had a spinnaker up again within twenty-four hours of the accident, we were not really racing properly until a week later. The psychological effect made people lose interest in pushing the boat. And it was noticeable that afterwards, sitting down to a meal, when the boat just lurched a little, all would stop talking and start hanging on. The casualties were: two out with broken ribs, one torn shoulder, one concussed, one aggravation of an old back-injury and Roberto's injured leg. The damage to the boat was: starboard mizzen lower shroud broken, binnacle and starboard compasses lost; cover of port cockpit seat broken; stern pulpit twisted; lights on the mainmast twisted, wind gauge vane broken off; window in main cabin broken; deckhead in after cabin and work-room torn; four out of five radios out; depth-finder out, sheet-winch handles and shackles lost; mizzen spinnaker and No. 2 mizzen staysail lost; horseshoe lifering and man-overboard pole and light lost; mizzen staysail halyard broken, dodger frame bent and dodger torn; steering wheel buckled, many other pieces of gear and food written off.'

Alan Gurney-designed *Great Britain II* off Cape Town's Table Mountain at the start of the second leg. She was to complete her second Whitbread ten days faster.

Despite this carnage, the crew recovered to win the leg on handicap and take the overall lead.

It was on the second leg that *Adventure*'s chances of winning the race on handicap evaporated when her rudder broke. The crew was forced to slow the boat so that she could be steered with the trim-tab on the back of the keel. When they arrived in Sydney, they were moored to a quarantine buoy awaiting immigration and Customs clearance. A case of champagne found its way on board and another of Cape brandy was unearthed from the bilges. By the time the night was through, and the boat and crew cleared, there were not too many sober crew on board. *Adventure* had a 'hand' berthing at the jetty at the Royal Australian Naval Sailing Association, RANSA, headquarters and the race chairman refused to go aboard until the boat was fit for him. Tabarly won line honours, his re-masted *Pen Duick VI* setting a noon-to-noon record of 305 miles, to beat Blyth's *Great Britain II* into Sydney by nine hours. This victory was short-lived, however, for soon after starting from Sydney she lost her mainmast again, to end this promising French challenge.

This left Blyth and his paratroopers to set the pace for the remainder of the race – though at considerable cost. Midway to the Horn, Bernard Hosking, who had survived one man-overboard incident during the first stage after being knocked over by the spinnaker pole, fell again. A sail-tie he was pulling on suddenly gave way and he lost his footing. The crew made two triangular-patterned searches over a four-hour period, but never again sighted Hosking or the horseshoe lifebelts they had thrown to him.

No one will ever forget the Rio de Janeiro stop-over, even if the yacht club was way above their station in life. It was carnival time and, as Leslie Williams remembered, the world's greatest pickpockets were in action. He safety-pinned a large denomination note into his trouser pocket only to find most of it gone, clipped away from the safety-pin while he enjoyed the sights and sounds of the Mardi Gras.

GB II, as the yacht was affectionately termed, went on to carry Chay and his crew to a line-honours victory back at Portsmouth in 144 days, but it was Mexico's Ramon Carlin and his *Sayula II*, finishing with a frayed forestay, which won the principal Whitbread trophy. The Royal Navy's *Adventure* was second followed by André Viant's French yacht *Grand Louis*.

Profile

Ramon Carlin

Ramon Carlin was born on the wrong side of the tracks, but was generally secretive about his background. Mexico is a strange country where the 'haves' have enormous amounts of money and the 'have nots' live in abject poverty. Ramon was born into the 'have nots' but was determined not to remain there.

He was, from the start, an entrepreneur and like the majority of his genre he began with almost nothing. He started by buying a set of cutlery from a five-and-dime store and then hawked his 'stock' door-to-door until he had sold it for considerably more than he had paid for it. With the money, he bought more and carried on around the streets of Mexico City, selling, selling, selling.

From cutlery, it was a short step into pots and pans and other household utensils; items that everybody wanted. He began to employ other kids to sell his wares and, at the same time, started to buy in bulk, cheaper than he had been able to buy elsewhere, and increase his profit margin to pay the commission to his salesmen.

The great divide in Mexico is not simply one of money, although this has a great deal to do with it. The privileged society in Mexico is one in which there are barriers of class and breeding and very little middle class. At the Azteca Stadium, where the World Cup soccer final has been played twice, there are two tiers of private boxes with their own bathrooms with gold taps. In 1966 they were changing hands at $100,000, while less than a quarter of a mile away there were families living in caves in the lava.

Despite having accumulated considerable wealth from his entrepreneurial activities – at the time of the 1973/74 race, Carlin had his own factories manufacturing washing machines and other household goods – the divide was still in evidence. He was not accepted by those of a similar financial standing because of his background, and yet his enormous wealth was a barrier to acceptance in the places where he had grown up. He saw yachting as a means of entry into at least one part of Mexican society.

His first *Sayula* was a Cal 40, (the type of boat originally used for the Congressional Cup), which he raced more in San Diego than Mexico, although he did enter her in the Ensanada and Cabo San Lucas races. The boat also had a berth in Acapulco where he obtained his professional hand, a man who so resembled the Mexican film star Cantinflas that he was called Cantis. Cantis had once been a cliff diver, plunging off the cliffs into the sea for tourist dollars.

It was in California that Carlin met Irving Loube, a man who was to have a distinct influence. Loube had owned a series of crack racing boats, including the Admiral's Cup yacht, *Bravura*. Carlin still sought acceptance into Mexican society. To achieve that properly he felt he had to complete some feat which would see him recognised internationally, and thus ingratiate himself with the President. The Whitbread Race was the obvious (to him) event in sailing.

He asked Loube what type of boat he should buy for the race and Irv replied: 'A strong boat.' When Carlin queried what a strong boat was, Loube walked him down the dock and pointed to a Swan 48 and said, '*That* is a strong boat.' Carlin telephoned Nautor in Finland and ordered a Swan 55, but when he went to Pietarsaari to confirm the order, he discovered the workforce engaged on a newer and bigger model, the Swan 65.

It was everything he wanted and he had to have one. But there he ran into a minor hurdle. The production was booked for months ahead and there would not be time for one to be built to race in the Whitbread.

It was the sort of problem which had dogged Carlin all his working life and he set about swapping places on the waiting list with someone else. The hull was already in mould and the dark-green colour already committed. The only deviation from the standard yacht was that *Sayula II* had guardrail stanchions of thicker-walled tube. Butch Dalrymple-Smith, one of the 'gringos' in the crew, writes of him,

'During the race, Ramon's preoccupation was to see that everyone was happy and well fed. We averaged six bottles of wine per day all round the course. Ramon was virtually teetotal, although I think he took a glass of wine from time to time. The rest of us consumed an enormous quantity of spirits (averaging almost a bottle a day) and about the same quantity of beer as most of the others for whom it was their sole source of liquor. I remember on one leg, it was fourteen cases (twenty-four cans to a case).

The food was good too because we had a deep-freeze, so steaks, hamburgers, chicken, etc lasted well on each leg. He really looked after us well. He even *bought* beer for one leg because he felt we preferred it to the stuff Whitbreads were handing out free. The wine was selected with equal care.

Ramon did not come on deck often, preferring to let us get on with it. I think, maybe, twice he came on deck all excited and

Ramon Carlin, Mexican millionaire owner of the ketch-rigged Swan 65 *Sayula II*, and his wife Paquita celebrate winning the first Whitbread on Easter Day 1974.

RAMON CARLIN

Ramon Carlin and the *Sayula II* crew, before the start in Portsmouth; a mix of Mexicans and top ocean-racing 'gringos' including Butch Dalrymple-Smith, who later went to work with designer Ron Holland. Opposite: *Sayula II.*

started yelling for different things to be done. When he was in this state, he forgot all his English and shouted in Spanish, so that the 'hired guns' would stand around doing nothing and the Mexicans would rush around like mad. But this only sticks in my memory because it was so out of character, and so very rare. He never held any animosity afterwards.

Most of the time he used to organise things below, keep up with Ray Conrady's navigation and generally ensure that the boat was being sailed right.

A typical cameo is that in the Southern Ocean – really freezing and blowing like stink – you come off the deck absolutely drained of energy. As well as serving everyone a drink, he would wait until everyone had turned in, then go round picking up foul-weather gear, towels, boots and hang them up to dry for us.'

It was typical of Ramon that he didn't insure the boat. His attitude was that there was only one thing worth insuring the boat for – a total loss – and that he would then probably not survive to make the claim. His crew only discovered this as they approached the finish at Southsea with only fourteen of the nineteen strands holding in the forestay. In the Southern Ocean capsize, the damage to the radios and other repairs cost $11,000, only a fraction more than the insurance premium would have been for the race (times have changed).

The crew worked hard to make the boat look good. Before they arrived in Sydney, they attempted to make the boat sparkle, stripping the lashings from the forward guardrails and polishing the stanchions. They even had a man over the side in a bosun's chair polishing the glassfibre. The woodwork below was polished with wax and even the unused halyards were stripped from the mast and the surplus food ditched. Ramon hated it; he wanted his boat to look as if it had just battled through enormous hardships to get there.

Carlin's organisation was superb. Two days before the finish of a leg, he would make a list of all the food and drink needed for the next and ask the crew about their preferences. He also made lists of repairs and maintenance required. The day after docking, the food list would be left with a victualler with the instructions to deliver it, the meat pre-frozen, to the boat two days before the start of the next leg. The crew would quickly sort through the work-list and then have time free to enjoy themselves in port. Carlin had ensured that they would have more time than the others to do so.

Once the race was over, two of the crew helped deliver the boat part of the way to Acapulco. One left the boat in St Thomas and the other in Panama, so that Carlin could take his own boat home to a civic reception from the President. Carlin, the achiever, had achieved exactly what he had set out to do – win the Whitbread and win a place in the country's society.

7208
BL 333

Profile

Chay Blyth

Atlantic rower, *Observer* Round Britain and Transatlantic Race-winner and a three-time circumnavigator, two of them as a Whitbread competitor, Chay Blyth is, perhaps, Britain's best-known yachtsman. He is certainly its most controversial. The former 'Red Beret' paratroop sergeant has never been a man to stand on ceremony – or bow to the privileged ranks within yachting. Though treated as something of an outcast by the British establishment, his exploits have risen above their heads, winning the admiration of a much wider and more appreciative audience.

'To begin with, I knew nothing about sailing – I couldn't even navigate,' recalls the Scot. ' I saw it as an adventure, with the ocean providing one of the last great challenges. I thought I would teach myself as I went along – and did, which got up the noses of the bar-room gin-and-tonic brigade, because it destroyed the cosy image that sailing is elitist and takes a lifetime to learn.'

Blyth's association with the sea began in 1966 with a row across the Atlantic with fellow paratrooper John Ridgway. 'We were after £180 to cover the cost of building our 20ft boat,' he remembers of those first efforts at raising money and sponsorship. 'We didn't approach any companies because, believe me, everyone in the press was convinced we were going to die. Instead, we went to our bank and were laughed out of court for asking about an overdraft facility. It was only after a friend agreed to act as guarantor, that we got the money at all.'

The pair made it across in 92 days, but not without a good deal of press speculation that Ridgway, the captain, had pulled rank, making his sergeant row the entire way. 'No, that's not true. John did row, but only when I was cooking,' Chay jokes now. 'Rank never came into the picture. In the paras you are taught to rely on each other. We had a good bond throughout the voyage – until we stepped ashore.' It was only afterwards that rank and privilege pervaded once more, and the memory of an invitation for Ridgway to address one of the Royal yacht clubs, with the rider: 'And will you be bringing your sergeant with you?', still rankles. Later Ridgway was to be awarded the OBE but Blyth only the BEM

Blyth's next exploit was to enter the *Sunday Times* Golden Globe challenge to be first to sail around the world non-stop alone. The motive, perhaps, was that Ridgway had already entered, plus the offer of a free yacht which later proved totally unsuitable for riding the Southern Ocean storms. Sponsorship was also a problem. One company sent down a naval officer to test him on his navigation and seamanship skills – he failed – and Blyth turned down a £12,000 offer by a newspaper because they wanted to change the name of his boat. 'That was a silly mistake – and biggest single lesson I have learned,' he says now of that lost opportunity.

Blyth was forced to throw in the towel shortly after rounding the Cape of Good Hope, and returned home to plot a fresh adventure. Impressed by the *Sunday Times* concept, he proposed to sail around the world the opposite way. 'I guess I was naive. I didn't realise there was any big difference between what Knox-Johnston had achieved and going round the other way against the prevailing winds and currents,' Blyth admits now candidly.

British Steel was his first call for sponsorship. 'That was something of a coup. My approach coincided with their plans to launch a steel marketing campaign,' he recalls. Surprisingly, what impressed British Steel most was Blyth's failure in the *Sunday Times* race. 'In truth, it would have been easier to die than give up, and there are a lot of people in sailing who believe you should go on regardless. I have never taken that view. If you are not winning and something breaks, then it is better to give up than finish at the back of the fleet – or worse. They knew that if there was a crisis, the promotion was unlikely to end with my death.'

Blyth left Southampton in the Robert Clark-designed 59ft steel ketch *British Steel* on 18 October 1970 and returned to the Hamble River 292 days later, having steered by hand for more than 20,000 miles after his self steering was smashed off Cape Horn.

The Times described the voyage as 'the most outstanding passage ever made by one man alone' and the thousands who came to greet his return left the gin-and-tonic brigade spluttering into their glasses.

The next challenge was to be the Whitbread; sponsorship fell into his lap like some fortuitous apple. 'I had been talking with an oil company and was convinced they were going with us,' recalls Blyth.

'While waiting for a final answer, we went out to stay with friends in the Bahamas and were invited to stay with Jack Hayward. We got on very well.'

'Union' Jack Hayward is the ex-patriot philanthropist who owns half of Grand Bahama island and has spent much of his life

Chay Blyth CBE, BEM, yachtsman, adventurer and twice a competitor in the Whitbread, with *Great Britain II* in 1973 and again, in the renamed *United Friendly*, in 1981.

British Soldier finishing the 1973/74 Race at Southsea. Earlier, the 56ft ketch had been sailed non-stop single-handed the 'wrong way' round the world by Blyth.

and money promoting Britain. It was he who rescued Brunel's first iron steamship SS *Great Britain* from a watery grave in the Falklands, bought Lundy Island, the wildlife sanctuary in the Bristol Channel for the nation and, for many years, sponsored Rachel Hayhoe's English women's cricket team on foreign tours.

Blyth could not believe that a private individual could sponsor such a huge commitment, and when the oil crisis put paid to his petro-dollars, Hayward was not the first name that came to mind as a fresh source. But it did to Frank Allen, Blyth's friend and mentor, who quietly rang the financier to tell him of Blyth's plight. Four days later, Hayward put in a transatlantic call to Chay and surprised him by saying: 'Why don't we go for it – build the boat.'

It was the start of a remarkable relationship. 'Over the years, we built three boats and never did have a contract. Jack made a huge impact on my life,' reflects Chay now.

Great Britain II won line honours in that first Whitbread race, setting a bench-mark record for the circumnavigation of 144 days. But the loss of fellow paratrooper Bernie Hosking in the Southern Ocean had a marked effect on Blyth. 'In the paras we were trained to cope with death. It is an occupational hazard,' says Blyth. 'That doesn't mean life is cheap. But we were taught to be realistic and get on with the job when all hope for one of our number is lost. Hosking fell overboard into waters that were close to freezing and the conditions were rough. His life expectancy could be counted in minutes, yet we searched for hours and never even saw the cushions, drogue or lifebuoys we had thrown over to mark his position. Our decision to carry on in the race was one we had all been trained to make, and one that Bernie himself would have wanted us to take.'

There were lighter sides to the race. When the project was first announced, Blyth was overwhelmed with applicants from within the paratroop regiments. Sailing experience was not a prerequisite, but keenness and commitment were. Blyth weeded out the less interested by setting them difficult tasks. One initiative test was for each applicant to get to Leeds town hall early one Saturday morning. 'They came from all over the country, Northern Ireland and Germany expecting a weekend of training,' says Chay. They were quite surprised to find me standing on the steps with a clipboard merely ticking their names off and telling them they were off duty. The only valid excuse I would accept was their death. Any who did not show up were struck off.' He laughs now at his crude selection system.

During the race itself, Blyth came in for some criticism from his crew and ribbing from competitors for his preference for curries. 'We experienced two problems during that first leg,' he answers defensively. 'The first was that two pipes leading into our water tanks cracked and all our drinking water seeped away. As most of our food was dehydrated, we had to distil sea water. That meant using up our gas supplies which led in turn to a shortage for cooking. Then we fell into a large hole for three or four days and ended up on starvation rations – which was curry!'

Leaving Sydney, bound for Cape Horn, Blyth and his paratroopers had a close escape. 'We were heading south and ended up having to sail through Bass Strait,' Blyth recalls. 'I told the duty officer to call me up once the lighthouse marking the end of the Strait was in view. I didn't sense the urgency with his first call, but there was no mistaking it after I told him I would be up once I had dressed. I ran up the companionway to find the lighthouse right above us! As one crew was shouting "breakers to starboard" I was calling for all hands on deck with their lifejackets. I was sure we were going on the rocks. Miraculously, we found a passage between the lighthouse and the reef, but it must have been close.'

It is a credit to Blyth that *Great Britain II* is the only yacht that competed in each of the first five Whitbread races. Rob James captained a crew of paying passengers in the second race in 1977/78, and Blyth returned to skipper the yacht, then renamed *United Friendly* for the 1981/82 event.

It was not one of his most memorable voyages, though his name alone brought more than its fair share of publicity even though some of the stories were at his expense. In Cape Town, Blyth's name was the first to come to mind with one rival skipper when he was caught by a devoted mother, in bed with her daughter. 'What's your name?' she screamed to the unseen male hiding under the sheets. 'Chay Blyth,' he retorted before grabbing his trousers and making a run for it.

Ten days later, as the *United Friendly* crew struggled into port at the end of the first leg, the irate mother was waiting on the dockside to give the real Blyth a piece of her mind. 'I didn't have a clue what she was talking about,' he laughs now.

In Auckland, the next port of call, Blyth had his leg pulled for the short amount of time he had spent on deck. The crew had presented him with a new pair of tartan slippers for Christmas.

'He would never come on deck if there was the slightest chance of getting his slippers wet. The furthest he would come was to poke his head out through the hatch so it seemed appropriate to order a new pair because we expected him to have worn his own out by the half-way stage,' laughed Jeff Houlgrave, his No. 2 onboard.

The crew played another memorable prank on their skipper during the third stage too. Blyth, who takes Hogmanay as seriously as any other true Scot, organised a party onboard complete with taped piper playing in the haggis and a fair few drams of Scotland's best. His crew knew that nature would call him on deck at some point and had worked out a surreptitious signal to call those on watch down through the forward hatch moments before he appeared through the main companionway. Thankfully, the disbelief on his face when he found the boat was sailing through the Southern Ocean under spinnaker without a soul on deck was caught for us all to share by the BBC film cameraman within the crew. 'It was one of the few times during the voyage that he ever rushed to take over the wheel,' Houlgrave chuckled when telling of their escapade on arrival at Mar del Plata.

If that race failed to stimulate Blyth's competitive instincts, he remained a master of publicity, gaining as many column inches in the London dailies as the eventual winner.

The 65ft ketch *Flyer* in which Cornelis van Rietschoten won the second Whitbread race.

FIRST

Chapter Two

The 1977 • 78 Race

Despite the loss of three lives, the crews who returned from the first race judged it to be such a success that preparations for another began almost immediately. With three years to plan, several owner/skippers commissioned designs to take advantage of the many lessons learned during the first Whitbread. Les Williams teamed up with Robin Knox-Johnston, the first man to have sailed around the world alone, to build the 79ft varnished *Heath's Condor*, designed by John Sharp and paid for by the then anonymous maxi-yacht owner Bob Bell. Peter Blake was recruited once more as watch-leader.

Against them, Rob James, now working for Chay Blyth, returned with *Great Britain II* and sixteen raw recruits who had each paid £4,000 for the adventure. Other yachts to return included the Royal Navy's *Adventure*, sailed by a rotating crew that included Ian Bailey-Willmot, (race director for the 1993/94 event), who was to skipper the third stage around Cape Horn. Tabarly's famous *Pen Duick III*, which had competed on the final stage of the previous Whitbread, returned under the new name of *Gauloises II*, skippered by one of Tabarly's disciples, Eric Loizeau. Tabarly himself was cruising the Pacific, but planned to join the fleet at Auckland which had replaced Sydney as the half-way staging post. His appearance was to present the race with its first controversy. *Pen Duick VI* carried a keel cast from spent uranium, an exotic material barred under the latest rules that came into force on 1 January that year, three days after the fleet would leave for Cape Horn. Natural justice suggests that if a yacht measured correctly on the day of the start, then subsequent changes to the rules could be ignored. That was the line taken by the committee but, while checking over the details, they noted that the expiry date on the measurement certificate Tabarly carried on the yacht had run out, thus invalidating her entry. The Frenchman claimed that his national authority had re-issued the certificate, but with Paris celebrating Christmas and the New Year, there was no one to confirm this.

The affair was blown up out of all proportion, and painted by Tabarly's supporters as another skirmish in the long-running Anglo-French conflict that began with the battle of Agincourt and culminated with Charles de Gaulle's refusal to allow Britain's entry to the European Common Market. Politics and sport never mix, but the committee did its best by allowing the French yacht to start as a provisional entry, while Knox-Johnston kept Tabarly's interest focused by wagering a bottle of champagne on the outcome of the last stage, by which time the Frenchman was no longer on the official entry list.

Three teams followed Ramon Carlin's success with Swan 65s. Pierre Fehlmann brought, *Disque d'Or*, the first Swiss entry to the race and Clare Francis became the first female skipper aboard *ADC Accutrac*. The sloop-rigged *King's Legend*, owned by Nick Ratcliffe and crewed by a number of hot-shots from the offshore racing world, including the American Skip Novak, made up the trio. *Traité de Rome*, the former German Admiral's Cup yacht *Pinta*, now skippered by Philippe Hanin, brought together a rotating crew from each of the Common Market states that included Ireland's Harold Cudmore who stepped aboard for the last leg back from Rio.

From France, Bernard Deguy brought the 59ft André Mauric-designed sloop *Neptune* to compete on almost equal terms with the veteran *33 Export*, now in the capable hands of another young Frenchman, Alain Gabbay. The fifth French entry was Jean-Michel Viant's 65ft ketch *Japy Hermes*.

From Britain, John Ridgway, who had rowed across the Atlantic with Blyth and entered the first Golden Globe solo circumnavigation challenge, gained sponsorship from Debenhams to enter a Bowman 57 racer/cruiser, and Corrado di Majo's 54ft *B&B Italia* ensured a Mediterranean interest.

The Netherlands produced two entries, both of them unknown to the outside racing world. Dirk Nauta's 63ft multi-chined alloy yacht *Tielsa* pursued the adventure aspect, a legacy of the first race, but for Cornelis 'Conny' van Rietschoten, there was only one objective – to win. This forty-nine-year-old Dutchman had just sold the family electronics firm and turned to Sparkman & Stephens to improve the design of their Swan 65 built by Nautor. The result was

***ADC Accutrac*, Clare Francis' Swan 65 ketch in 1977/78. Opposite: *Heath's Condor*.**

07
707

Flyer, a 65ft alloy ketch built by Wolter Huisman with a waterline length, dictating her maximum displacement speed, some two foot nine inches longer than the Nautor production yachts.

Unlike many other entries which suffered from a lack of preparation time, including the Williams/Knox-Johnston entry *Heath's Condor* whose crew were still putting the finishing touches to the yacht's experimental carbon-fibre mast on the eve of the start, *Flyer*'s crew completed two transatlantic crossings to prove their design. Eventually, it was this attention to detail that set the Dutch crew apart from the rest.

First to falter was *Heath's Condor* when her mast suddenly broke in three places, three thousand miles from Portsmouth, to end the second competitive challenge from Williams. Knox-Johnston, who alternated as skipper, organised for a new mast to be air-freighted out to Monrovia. They arrived in Cape Town just in time to compete on the second stage.

By that time *Flyer* had already begun to dominate the race, winning both line and handicap honours into Cape Town; the Dutch yacht's closest threat being Ratcliffe's *King's Legend*.

Stage two, this time to Auckland, would again prove to be the toughest. One of the first to suffer was *Gauloises II* which broke a new rudder, fitted specially for the Southern Ocean. Her disappointed crew put into Port Elizabeth to replace it with the original foil but, though completing the work within a day, they then faced completely different weather to the rest of the fleet and never caught up.

Line honours went to the re-rigged *Heath's Condor*, Peter Blake steering her in to a hero's welcome at his home port. The yacht had been lucky, however, that disaster had not struck a second time. Mid-way across the Southern Ocean, crewman Bill Abram had been flipped overboard by the lazy spinnaker sheet. The crew had some trouble turning round. First the spinnaker had to be taken down and trailing sheets brought in. When it came to engaging the engine, the blades of the propeller refused to open. By now the crew had lost sight of Abram. After sailing back to where a flock of albatrosses was circling overhead, they found their man, cold but alive, within ten minutes. Aboard *Great Britain II*, crewman Nick Dunlop and his skipper Rob James were caught up in the loop of the spinnaker afterguy during a spinnaker take-down, some one thousand miles west of Tasmania. As they began to haul the sail in, *Great Britain II* was knocked broadside to the seas and part of the sail fell in the water. 'Nick and I rushed to the lee rail, got our hands on the sail and started to pull,' James recalled.

'Nick was kneeling and I was standing by his right shoulder. We lost our grip on the cloth and the rest of the sail rushed past us and disappeared astern. It was still attached by five ropes and one or more of these had formed a loop on the deck at exactly the point where Nick and I found ourselves. The loop snatched tight around Nick's waist and my knees, and I think I had a hand in there as well. It pulled tighter and tighter.

I yelled for a knife. Nick was sick and then lost consciousness, his torso hanging back limply from the top loop. We had been dragged down the deck, breaking a stanchion, and were coming up against the rigging. I was still screaming for help when Ian Worley arrived on the scene to cut every rope in sight. There was so much weight on them, they parted like paper. The relief that I was free and could stand was immense.'

But the situation was nasty. Dunlop remained unconscious and the spinnaker was flying free from the masthead at the end of a 100ft halyard. For the first time James regretted not shipping a doctor. As the skipper organised the safety of the yacht, the crew brought up the saloon table to act as a stretcher while the cold spray flying across the deck helped to bring Dunlop round.

'We managed to get Nick below which was not easy because he was in a lot of pain,' James recounted. 'We eventually had him wedged between the seat and the table on the saloon floor but all attempts to move him further were halted by his agonised cries. I cut away his clothes and could see no visible damage so we covered him with sleeping bags and filled two empty whisky bottles with hot water to try and warm him up.'

A few minutes later it was time for the daily inter-yacht radio schedule and James was able to seek advice. *Condor*'s doctor advised them to give Nick a shot of morphine and get him on his back in a bunk. The doctor remained in contact for several days as Dunlop slowly pulled through the ordeal.

The race for the handicap lead remained nail-bitingly close. *Flyer* had set out from Cape Town with a two-hour advantage over *King's Legend* but, staying cautiously high of the Roaring Forties, had soon dropped three hundred miles behind the British sloop. Half-way across, however, delamination problems at the rudder-post struck *King's Legend*. Her disappointed crew, now pumping on an hourly basis and reporting their position and situation every six hours in case the hull failed completely, were forced to slow their pace.

Bill 'Lord of the Horn' Porter taking a noon sight on *King's Legend* 1977/78. Opposite: *Tielsa*, Dirk Nauta's first Whitbread entry in the 1977/78 race.

At the finish, *Flyer*, which had also been slowed by a broken main boom, lost just forty-five minutes of her earlier lead.

Later, *Flyer* also ran into spectacular trouble shortly after rounding Cape Horn, eighteen hours behind *Great Britain II*. Skipper Conny van Rietschoten later related the experience.

'Three hours after passing close-hauled between Norta and Diego Island, we spotted the Horn – a sight we had sailed halfway round the world to see and one that none of us would easily forget. *Flyer* had beaten *Condor* round by twelve hours and it had all been straightforward sailing: I couldn't believe our luck. Then, as if the Cape had read my thoughts, black clouds rolled across to mark another frontal passage. 'More wind' I remarked rubbing my hands with glee 'That's what we need to keep pace with *Pen Duick*.' But I didn't reckon on how much. The first squall to hit was a fifty-knot blast, and swinging to a completely different angle, it caught us with all sail up and the boom lashed down on the opposite side. It hit with such ferocity that there was no time to think and the boat crashed over in a chinese gybe. I was letting out the mizzen sheet at the time and just held on, suspended in mid-air as the yacht lurched over. Rod was thrown bodily across the deck to land in the scuppers but everyone else managed to cling on somehow. For the first time *Flyer* lay trapped, pinned down by the weight of water in her sails and the wind that blasted in over the boom. Struggling to get a foothold back on deck, I caught a glimpse of the mainmast dipping beneath the waves.

Jerry Dijkstra clambered up to release the preventer on the main boom. Aedgard Koekebakker let slip the leeward running backstay, and the sail crashed across, smacking the water. The

Robin Knox-Johnston at the wheel of *Heath's Condor* in the second leg of the 1977/78 race. Opposite: Nick Ratcliffe's sloop-rigged Swan 65 *King's Legend* thrashes her way through the Southern Ocean on a reach.

mizzen was also caught, the preventer jammed in its cleat by the strain on it, so I tore at the halyard and wrenched the sail down. *Flyer* twitched like a boxer out cold. We all wondered if she would beat the count, for water was pouring down through the open hatch. Slowly she stirred, and swinging back on her feet, unsteadily at first, shook herself down then waited patiently for us to gather our wits.

As the fleet headed north, drama hit the French yacht *33 Export*. A green wave running down the deck washed crewman Eric Letrosne into the lifelines. They saved him from falling overboard but the impact resulted in a badly broken femur. His leg had become jammed between the lee rail and liferaft. Skipper Alain Gabbay also broke his thumb in the incident but, so far from land, no immediate outside assistance was available. *Japy Hermes*, the nearest Whitbread yacht with a doctor aboard, made the rendezvous, but with the swell too large to transfer either Letrosne, by now suffering secondary shock and pain, or the medic by liferaft, Dr Jean-Louis Sabarly swam across – an action that later won him an award.

Once Sabarly was aboard, *33 Export* headed for Rio Grande to drop off the injured crew-member before continuing in the race. By Rio, the margin between *Flyer* and *King's Legend* had opened up to fifty-nine hours.

For some, Rio also provided new dimensions in thrills, as Eve Bonham from *ADC Accutrac* found. After a few bus rides round the Brazilian city, she spoke animatedly of the quality of vehicle-handling: 'Broaching off Cape Horn was child's play compared with one bus I went in,' she said.

But the inefficiencies and corruption in South America almost brought it all to naught. New sails to replace *Flyer*'s tattered wardrobe were lost in transit and it was only after a last-minute bribe to Customs officials that the offending bags were found and cleared before the re-start. The backhanders necessary to get anything done in Brazil left a bad taste in many mouths but the final nail that was to seal Rio's fate as a stop-over port was delivered during a party at the Iate Clube do Rio de Janeiro.

The incident, which started with an impromptu conga led by Clare Francis, ended with the riot police flailing truncheons and firing tear-gas as two hundred or more crews wove an uneven course into the Club's swimming pool.

With new sails and fresh rigging *Flyer*'s lead proved too great to overcome, for though *King's Legend* led all the way home, van Rietschoten and his crew dogged her wake throughout, returning to Portsmouth an hour and twenty minutes later to take the principal prize.

The raw recruits aboard *Great Britain II* didn't do too badly either. Though *Condor* was first home to claim the champagne bet from Tabarly, Rob James and his crew not only won overall line honours, but posted a new race record of 134 days; ten days inside the time set by Chay Blyth and his paratroopers four years earlier.

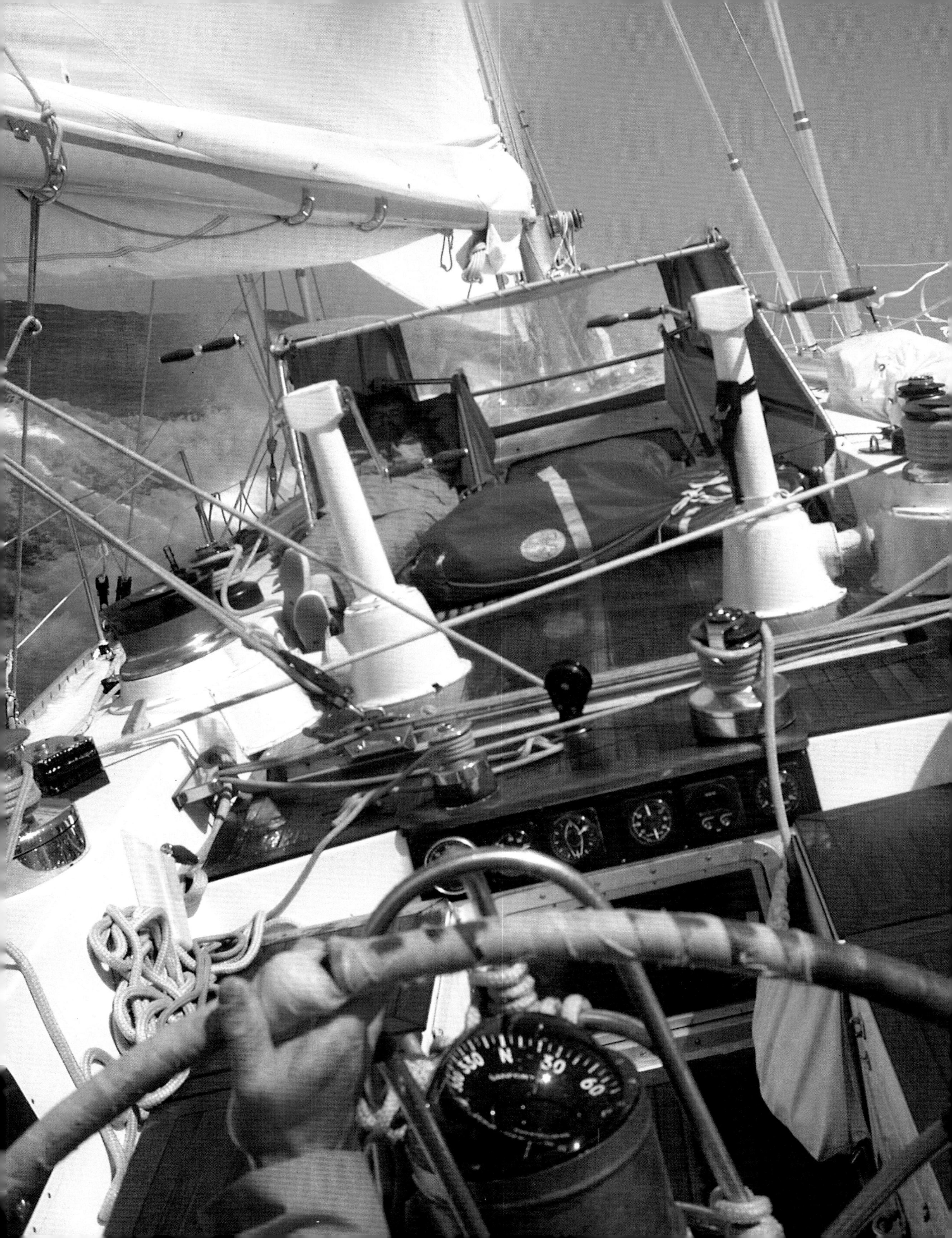

Profile

Rob James

After every major sporting event there is an award to the Man of the Match. Had there been one in April 1978, for the Whitbread Race, it might have been thought difficult to select an individual from the over two hundred participants. One man, however, stood head and shoulders above the others; the choice of nearly all the competitors and observers – Rob James, skipper of the 77 foot ketch, *Great Britain II*.

Who would have taken on the responsibility of racing with a charter crew in the first place, particularly deep in the Southern Ocean, where three people, including one from *GB II*, had lost their lives in the race four years before? Who would have accepted as crew-members many who had never sailed before with only one who had raced this type of offshore racer in their lives? Only a man of tremendous confidence in himself and in his ability to create a working crew from a hotch-potch of fare-paying passengers; Rob James did.

James' boyish looks, beneath a ginger thatch, belied his mature thirty-one years. He started sailing with his father at West Wittering, in a Heron, an 11ft 6in dinghy, a boat which they took to the Kingsmead Sailing Club. There, with a new suit of sails, Rob at the helm and his father crewing, they went to the front of the fleet. At fourteen, he went to Pangbourne Naval College, where a predecessor in the sailing team was the triple Olympic medallist, Rodney Pattisson. James left college at eighteen to join the merchant navy and after three years with P&O, during which time he gained his second mate's ticket, he went to Reading university to study mathematics and computer science.

It was a move that changed his attitude to the sport. Within eight months he was commodore of the university sailing club and a member of the team-racing squad.

After university, he went to ICL as a systems salesman where, as luck would have it, his regional manager was Ninian Eadie, who was starting to campaign a Soling three-man keel-boat for the 1972 Olympic trials. James said it would have been churlish of him to refuse the offer to be the spinnaker hand (doctor Frank Newton, later renowned for his work in sports medicine, was the foredeck man) and he spent eighteen happy months with the campaign.

At the beginning of 1973, James wrote to all the skippers entered for the first Whitbread, asking for a berth as a crew. The only one to make him an offer was Roddy Ainslie of *Second Life*. James' letter to him came as the result of reading an advertisement in *Yachting World* and he found that Ainslie was asking £3,000 to go towards the cost of chartering the 71ft yacht and for providing the food. To James this seemed reasonable enough, except that he was short of the £3,000. His father came to his aid with a loan. James went aboard as a watch-leader and the experience over the next eight months changed his life.

During that time he met Chay Blyth, who was planning to set up a charter business after the race and who asked James to join him, as a skipper. Even after 27,000 miles around the world, Rob was not sure and returned to ICL. He walked into the office at 0900 and two hours later tendered his resignation. He realised that he could no longer work for a large company – he had experienced freedom and instant responsibility and was not prepared to trade those for security. It was the work of a moment to phone Blyth and tell him that he was available.

James became a charter skipper, cruising and racing with *Great Britain II* and *British Steel*. In the winter of 1975/76 he skippered *British Steel* in the St Malo-Cape Town-Rio de Janeiro-Portsmouth Race; one which proved that racing with a charter crew was viable. On the quay at St Malo he met Naomi who became his wife six months later. She was later to sail *Express Crusader* around the world single-handed – the first woman ever to do so – at the same time that Rob was sailing *Great Britain II* in the Whitbread.

While Rob was in the Royal New Zealand Yacht Squadron one evening, during the race stop-over in Auckland, he received a link telephone call from Naomi who told him she was having trouble with her navigation after leaving Cape Town. She could not get her dead reckoning and her astro-navigation to equate. Rob returned to the bar laughing after putting his wife on the right track. It appeared that Naomi, after spending the first leg heading south, was now heading east. She had decided to measure her distance against the degrees of longitude on the bottom of the Mercator chart rather than, correctly, down the degrees of latitude on the side. It amused him greatly that she could make such a simple mistake.

With *Great Britain II* available in 1977, it made sense to Blyth and James to offer her for charter for the Round the World Race at a price of £4,000 per berth. There were many applicants of whom fourteen were selected. They had just five days' practice aboard the ketch before the race. Only Nick Dunlop, one of the three chosen as watch-leaders, had seen a spinnaker up in anger

Rob James at the helm of *Colt Cars GB* from which he was tragically lost off Salcombe in March 1984. James took a crew of amateurs around in *GB II* in 1977/78.

***Colt Cars GB*, Rob James' Round Britain Race-winning trimaran. Opposite: James' crew working on the stern of *Great Britain II* in Auckland during her second race.**

before. Ian Worley had sailed his own boat across the Atlantic. Henriques Zuleta had done the Tall Ships Race in a square-rigger and the Hon Quentin Wallop (later Earl of Portsmouth) had cruised his Ocean 75 but never raced it. Peter Waring owned a Hurley 24 family cruiser and Errol Woods had been cruising. Otherwise, their joint experience was nil.

By the time they reached Cape Town, three and a half days faster than Blyth and his paratroopers, they were a working crew. By the halfway stage at Auckland, they were among the best in the race. James said they learned fast and could not praise them enough. He would have taken them, he said, anywhere without a worry; their performance spoke for itself. The happy bunch of Corinthians beat the overall time of Blyth and his highly-trained paras by exactly ten days. Their performance was due to the leadership of Rob James.

Soon after that Whitbread Rob turned his attention to multihulls. His first major race was two months later, the 1,900-mile Round Britain Race with Chay Blyth in *Great Britain IV*, a 56ft trimaran designed and built by Derek Kelsall. They arrived nine hours behind the leader at Crosshaven, the first stop-over, as a leak into the forward third of the starboard float had slowed them dramatically. Once that was repaired, they overhauled the opposition and went on to win by twelve-and-a-half hours.

Rob bought a secondhand 31ft trimaran, *Jan of Santa Cruz*, a Dick Newick design, with which to race in the OSTAR, the *Observer* Single-handed Transatlantic Race, in 1980. Renamed *Boatfile*, she finished sixteenth ahead of many much bigger boats. By this time, Rob and Naomi were living in Crosshaven, close to designer Ron Holland, but it was John Shuttleworth who designed the next multihull, *Brittany Ferries GB*, that he was to race with Chay Blyth; a boat of which Blyth was to say, 'If we don't win with this boat, we'll never win.'

The 1981 two-handed transatlantic race proved to be a huge success for Rob, Chay and *Brittany Ferries GB*. They won by a huge margin of sixteen hours, by having a fast boat and never deviating very far from the rhumb line. The following year, she would have to be the boat that Rob had to beat to win the Round Britain Race and for that reason he felt that Shuttleworth was not the designer to use but instead went to Ron Holland with whom he collaborated over the design of *Colt Cars GB*.

The 60ft trimaran came into being because Michael Orr, the chief executive of Colt Cars in Britain, had decided to use it as a promotional vehicle and had secured the services of James to sail for him. Rob aimed to sail the boat with Naomi, and he and Holland bore this in mind as they planned an efficient sixty-footer – the largest size allowed for the 1984 OSTAR.

Colt Cars led into Crosshaven at the end of the first leg, by forty-eight minutes. On the next, to Barra, she dropped to third and was back up to second, behind *Brittany Ferries* at Lerwick; less than two hours separated them from Blyth and Peter Bateman. At Lowestoft, the gap was down to nineteen minutes and the two boats started in near calm and a foul tide. *Brittany Ferries* dragged her anchor and *Colt Cars* went into the lead before crossing the start line! The final leg was a classic with Spud Rowsell in *Exmouth Challenge* joining in the fray but Rob and Naomi held out to win by forty-three minutes.

Orr was delighted and shortly afterwards announced that he would sponsor a Whitbread entry with James as skipper. The project got underway with the formation of Mitsubishi Maritime to build the boat and Ron Holland appointed to design it. All seemed to be going well, with Rob overseeing the building and practising for the 1984 OSTAR with the trimaran, when disaster struck.

Early on the morning of 18 March 1982, Rob was dropping the mainsail of the trimaran off the entrance of Salcombe Harbour after a delivery trip from the Solent, when he stood on the netting between the main hull and the port float. The lashing to the hull gave way and Rob dropped into the sea. With only the jib up, *Colt Cars* was not easy to manoeuvre and the three-man, one-woman crew did all they could but it was some time before they were alongside the skipper. The cold had debilitated James and he needed help. Jeff Houlgrave tried to get him on board, but the motion of the trimaran prevented this and James slipped from his grasp and drowned. The sailing world had lost one of its great competitors through a simple but tragic accident.

GREAT
II

Cape Horn to Port – the Whitbread competitors' view of a sailor's most feared landmark.

Chapter Three

The 1981·82 Race

Heath's Condor had no sooner returned to Portsmouth, than Peter Blake was plotting in earnest for his own all-Kiwi entry for the next Whitbread in 1981. He had already written a letter to those in powerful places when he was in Auckland, after the line-honours win aboard *Heath's Condor*. It read:

'The rules read 'Cape Horn to Port'. Ever since my early yachting days racing a P class with the Takepuna Boating Club, one of my aims has been to round Cape Horn under sail. It has taken me over 100,000 miles of ocean racing and cruising to achieve, but what a highlight! After the frustrations of the first leg of the 1977/78 Whitbread Round the World Race from Portsmouth to Cape Town, the speeds and severe cold of the run to Auckland, the intensity and sheer pleasure of the New Zealand hospitality, and then the icebergs, hail and snow of 63 degrees south in the Southern Pacific Ocean, to approach and round Cape Horn under full sail aboard the 77ft sloop *Heath's Condor* meant a great deal to me, seeming to justify everything.

Flyer **leads the start out of Auckland in the 1981/82 race. Opposite: drying out at the end of a leg.**

The Royal Naval Sailing Association, which set up this race, talks about running another Round the World in 1981. We must have an entry of New Zealand design and construction, crewed solely by Kiwis. The time to begin such a project is now. Let's show the rest of the world what we really can do in the longest and toughest ocean race of the world.'

He won powerful support from key business and sailing friends, not least Sir Tom Clarke, head of Ceramco Industries in New Zealand and Peter Cornes who owned the Rothmans and Dunhill franchises. Cornes was one of three Auckland-based yachting enthusiasts who underwrote the construction of a 68ft Bruce Farr design, and with further support from a sailing-mad public, *Ceramco New Zealand* became the country's first national challenge.

Also to return was Cornelis van Rietschoten with a new 76ft Frers-designed *Flyer*, built to challenge *Great Britain II*'s record rather than handicap honours. They were among a record fleet of twenty-nine yachts from fifteen countries to congregate at Gosport for the third running of the race.

Great Britain II, entered in the name and colours of United Friendly Insurance, was also back with Chay Blyth in command once more. Les Williams built himself an 80ft maxi which underwent several name changes before finalising on *FCF Challenger*, and completing the challenge for line honours was Eric Tabarly's *Euromarché*.

The contrasting line-up for handicap honours was the most impressive yet. France and Italy headed the list numerically. Alain Gabbay took charge of the futuristic-looking 66ft Gilles Vaton design, *Charles Heidsieck III*; Philippe Poupon, the Le Figaro solo race-winner, arrived with the equally impressive 46ft *Mor Bihan* and André Viant, another of the first-race veterans, commissioned German Frers to design his 62ft *Kriter IX*. In contrast, Eric Loizeau went to Ron Holland for his similar-sized sloop *Gauloises III* and Philippe Schaff was handed the command of *33 Export*.

Compassionate officials within the Italian Yachting Federation kindly suspended a two-year ban imposed on Giorgio Falck for cheating his rating during his country's Admiral's Cup trials the previous year, in order for him to enter the purpose-built 51ft Frers-designed *Rollygo*. Other Italian entries included Roberto Vianello's 50ft *Ilgagomma*; Doi Malingri's 64ft *Save Venice* which became just as much a charitable cause as the race progressed; Beppe Panada's equally luckless *Vivanapoli* and a crew of scientists led by Claudio Stampi aboard *La Barca Laboratorio* which was to complete only one leg – the last. Italy also had an interest in the EC entrant *Traité de Rome* for it was skippered in this, her second, Whitbread by Antonio Chioatto.

Pierre Fehlmann again carried the aspirations of land-locked Switzerland with his 58ft Farr-designed *Disque d'Or III*

Charles Heidsieck, alias Champagne Charlie, racing at the SORC off Nassau as part of her work-up for the third Whitbread.

***Alaska Eagle*, formerly *Flyer*, re-rigged as a sloop, finishes the second leg in 1981/82. The transformation from ketch was ill advised. Opposite: the Frers-designed *Flyer* under spinnaker in the Southern Ocean.**

and Digby Taylor brought the rival Davidson-designed 50ft *Outward Bound* from New Zealand.

Padda Kuttel's South African-entered Swan 65 *Xargo III* provided the RNSA with a last-minute problem when the British government, which had recently signed the Gleneagles Agreement, found that it would be in breach of the new sporting code if the Royal Navy hosted the fleet at HMS Vernon once more. It proved once again that sport and politics are rare bed-fellows, but the RNSA expediently side-stepped the issue by moving their operations across Portsmouth Harbour to Camper & Nicholson's marina at Gosport.

The Scandinavian countries were represented for the first time with Norwegian Olympic yachtsman Peder Lunde skippering the Swan 57 *Berge Viking*, and two Swedish entries; a second Swan 57, *Scandinavian*, skippered by the SAS airline pilot Reino Engqvist, and *Swedish Entry*, a Norlin-designed 61-footer campaigned by Peder Silfverhielm. Rounding off the quartet was the Baltic 51 *Skopbank of Finland*, skippered by Kenneth Gahmberg.

Gustaaf Versluys entered his former Belgian Admiral's Cup yacht *Croky* to join Jean Blondiau's *European University of Belgium*. Representing Germany was the early Swan 55, *Walross III Berlin*, sailed by a rotating group of adventure-seekers.

More serious was the first US challenge, *Alaska Eagle* skippered by the former *King's Legend* crewman Skip Novak. Stories from the previous Whitbread race had intrigued and excited Neil Bergt, the owner of Alaska Airlines. He wanted to compete, but after leaving it too late to build, he bought Cornelis van Rietschoten's previous winner *Flyer*. He was then faced with the conflicting advice that so often divides winner from loser: change the boat from ketch to sloop and alter the stern sections, or run with Dutch advice, merely adding two feet to the mizzen mast. He chose the expensive American solution which added two feet to waterline length and a subsequent increase in wetted area, changed the rig from ketch to sloop, reducing her sail area, and paid the penalty. His crew did not realise the handicap until halfway round, but Bergt saw the writing on the wall at the end of the first leg. He stepped ashore at Cape Town to take over the ailing Western Airlines and was never seen again.

The first leg to Cape Town was dubbed by one yachting magazine as a 'destruction derby'. Three yachts, *Ceramco NZ*, *La Barca Laboratorio* and *Rollygo*, lost their rigs. *FCF Challenger*, and *Charles Heidsieck III* suffered serious rigging problems. *Bubblegum* broke a chainplate and also collided with a whale, losing steerage when the wire cables broke. *Traité de Rome* came perilously close to losing her entire skeg and rudder, and *Scandinavian* retired to Las Palmas with a long list of problems. Later her skipper committed suicide.

Vivanapoli's crew was arrested as spies after sailing into

Peter Blake's *Ceramco NZ* limps towards Cape Town after her dismasting on the first leg, 150 miles north of Ascension Island. Opposite: the jury-rigged mizzen mast on *Ceramco* which took them to eighteenth place on the leg.

Angolan territorial waters and skipper Beppe Panada did not help their cause by throwing the immigration officer overboard. After warning shots were fired, the entire crew was taken to Luanda where they spent seven days imprisoned. The delay cost them all chance of competing on the Southern Ocean stages, so they crossed the Atlantic to Mar del Plata, Argentina to re-join the fleet for the last leg home.

The most remarkable recovery, however, was that of *Ceramco*. After pressing *Flyer* for the first three weeks of the race, disaster struck her New Zealand crew one hundred miles from Ascension Island. 'Suddenly there was an almighty bang and a crash from up top. *Ceramco* came upright and slowed. I leapt for the hatch, yelling for the off-watch crew, and up I went,' said Blake who had suffered this nightmare once too often already.

An intermediate shroud had broken where the rod had been over-bent at a spreader tip which resulted in *Ceramco*'s mast folding in two places. The crew salvaged the fifty-foot top section and within twenty-four hours had a jury rig set utilizing cut down sails, a breadboard for the base-plate and a jockey pole as a sampson post below decks.

Remarkably, the crew managed to run 238 miles during one memorable twenty-four-hour period, a distance that even Tabarly could not better aboard the 73ft ketch-rigged *Euromarché*! Blake later recalled the experience.

'I didn't need to know what had happened. We'd broken the mast. I dashed up on deck. What a mess. The whole top half of the mast was over the side but still attached by internal halyards and wiring systems, plus the mainsail, jib and the headstay. Another section, probably twenty-feet long, was bent over and dangling down to the gunwhale. We were left with a sixteen-foot stump still in place.

It appeared that the port lower intermediate shroud had broken where it bent over the lower spreader. The mast didn't have to wait. The top section of the alloy mast, with all its attachments, was under the boat with the wind blowing *Ceramco* down on to it.

There were some shocked and glum faces about, but nobody hesitated. Fenders were put over the side to prevent hull damage by the section in the water. We used the motor – first making sure there were no lines under the propeller – to reverse the boat around until the spar and entanglements were to windward with *Ceramco* streaming to leeward of their danger. Then we used blocks and tackles slowly to winch the mast section back on board.

With everything back on deck – we salvaged the lot – we had only three bent stanchions to show for all the trouble. But we were 2,455 miles from Cape Town, as the crow flies, with only a sixteen-foot stump of a mast from which to hang a bare minimum of sail.

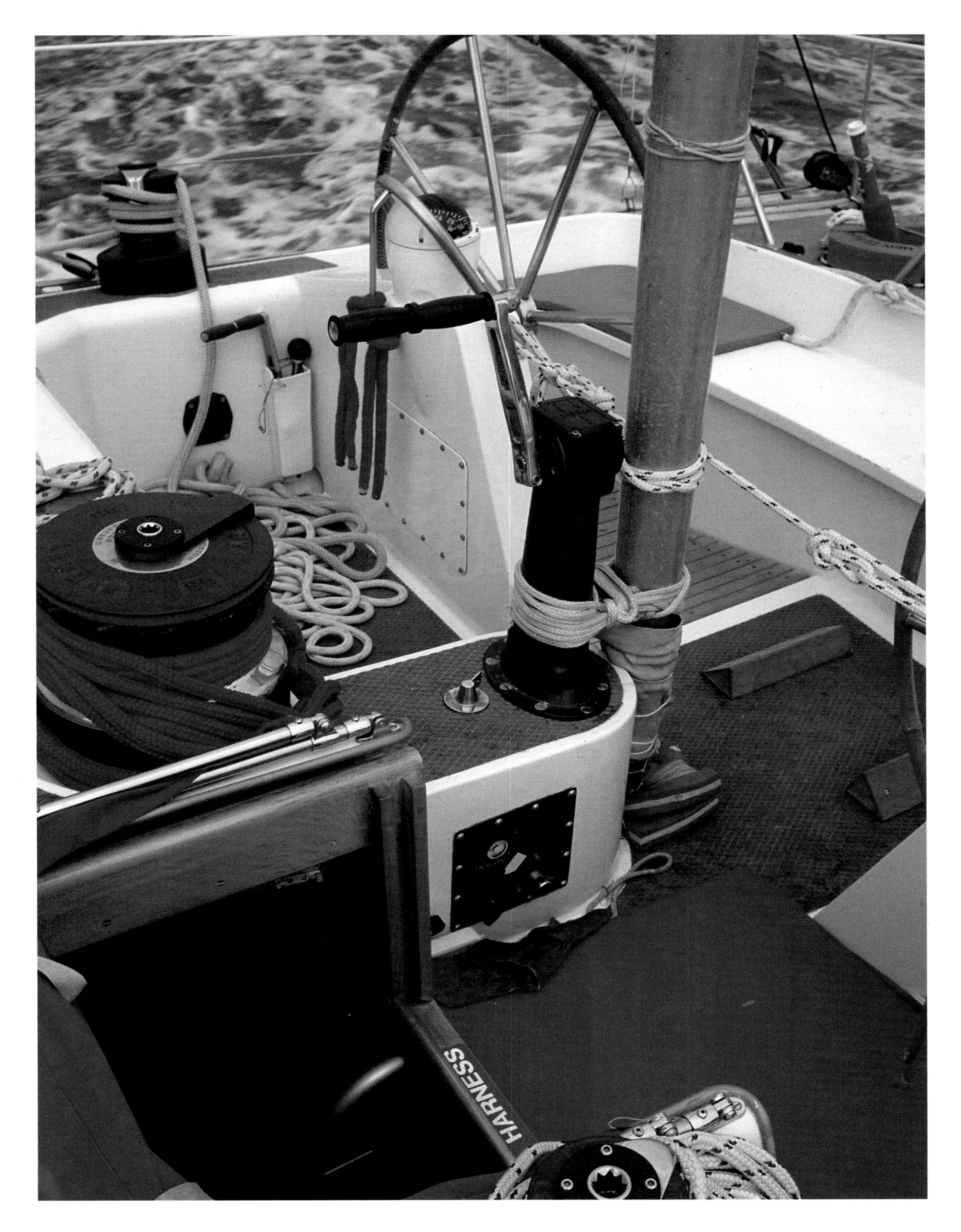
HARNESS

To get us moving again, while we took stock of the situation, we set the try sail and No. 6 jib on the stump and quickly were making four to five knots in the right direction. That was something. But it was daunting to think how far we had to go – most of it to windward if we contemplated the direct route.

We'd been lucky though. I shuddered when I thought what could have happened if someone had been to leeward, changing sheets or preparing for a headsail change, when it all came down.

The boat was unnaturally quiet; gloom and doom below and the mood wasn't helped by the necessity to let the outside world know what had happened. This, fortunately, posed no technical problem. Our big Sailor SSB radio worked through two whip aerials mounted on the stern. Things would have been a bit more difficult had we used the backstay as an aerial.

My first call was to my wife Pippa back in England. She burst into tears. Next I called Martin Foster in Auckland. My news was greeted by a stunned silence. Then it was the turn of Peter Montgomery of Radio New Zealand and Alan Sefton of the *Auckland Star*. These two had done so much for our project, they had a right to be the first media people to know. I had already informed the rest of the fleet on the chat show and sent a telex to the RNSA telling them we'd lost the mast but were continuing to Cape Town under jury rig.

Those chores out of the way, I assembled the crew and outlined our options. The direct route to Cape Town was out. *Ceramco* was in no condition to go sailing to windward. If we found we couldn't sail effectively, we could put in to Ascension Island, take on diesel, sail on as far as we could and then start the motor. This went down like the proverbial lead balloon.

We could also turn back and head for Monrovia, 800 miles to the north and have a new mast waiting there. But that would

Details of the jury-rigged mast of *Ceramco NZ*. Tackles taken supported the base to the toe rail – note 'Vonny's' bread board, borrowed for new duties as a mast step.

mean the end of the race for us. We would never get to Cape Town in time for the re-start to Auckland. I'd been to Monrovia before, when *Heath's Condor* lost her mast on the first leg of the 1977/78 Whitbread. We encountered all sorts of problems and, anyway, *Condor* had been 400 miles closer when we had to make our decision on that occasion.

Our best solution was to continue on to Cape Town by the downwind route, around the back (to the west) of the South Atlantic high-pressure systems, making as much speed as possible and having everything waiting for us to replace the rig when we got there.

We were right in the middle of the Atlantic anyway. The African coast, to the east, was to windward against the trade winds. We didn't really have much of a decision to make. But I got a big thrill from the crew reaction to this discussion. There was no question of pulling out to motor to Cape Town. We were still racing, albeit with our wings clipped. It would be up to good old Kiwi ingenuity to find ways of setting as much sail as possible to speed our journey. We'd be sailing anything from one thousand to two thousand miles further. But the trades had been blowing reasonably fresh and, with a few breaks, we could still make reasonable time. In our favour was the way the mast had broken. We had a forty-five-foot top section with all the attachments intact. If we could hoist this into place alongside the sixteen-foot bottom section, and hold it in position, there were all sorts of possibilities. We could still make it to Cape Town before some of the backmarkers.

I tried to wrap up the discussion on a light note saying: 'Now if anyone wants to get demoralized, come and see me and we'll get demoralized together.' There were no takers.

Left to my own thoughts, I reflected on our misfortune. Our estimates put *Flyer* 105 miles to the east of us. We'd been level pegging it down the South Atlantic and really beginning to look good on handicap.

Then there was the mast itself, slim in section and heavily-tapered at the top. It caused a lot of comment when it was stepped in Auckland and there were any number of waterfront experts prepared to bet it would come down. Well, it had – but through no fault in the spar or its engineering. The problem was a rigging failure. It wouldn't have mattered what size mast we'd had – we could have been using a telegraph pole. When that particular piece of the rigging failed, whatever we'd been using would have come down.

We'd had no problems from the spar in 16,000 miles of sailing. It had stood up like a tree trunk, even when we'd been caught napping by a fifty-knot squall leaving Auckland for the 1980 Sydney-Hobart. On that occasion we gybed all-standing with no runners on and finished up kicking on our side with the mast in the water. If it was going to go through any fault in its section size, design or engineering, it would have been then.

But there was little point in recriminations. Better now to devote all our thinking energy to getting out of this dilemma in the best possible shape, remembering always that there is still more than three-quarters of the race to run and a lot can happen to the opposition in more than 20,000 miles, particularly in the Southern Ocean where *Ceramco* has been designed and built to excel. Hopefully, we've now used up our ration of back luck.

For now, we're going back to what they used in Nelson's day. If we can rig the boat the way we intend, and get the same winds we've been having, we'll be doing seven to eight knots again. We won't be as hard on the wind as we'd like, but we will be able to steer a pretty good course and reach Cape Town not too far behind the others.'

The experience made Blake a hero at home and sharpened his crew's combative instincts to such a level that they pushed *Flyer* to the limits and beyond for the remainder of the race. For now they had Cape Town to heal old wounds. But even ashore there

Southern Ocean seas tower over the helmsman of van Rietschoten's *Flyer*. Opposite: it can be very wet on the leeward rail when adjustments are needed.

were some determined to live dangerously. Tim Burrel, a watch leader on *FCF Challenger*, set the first of two Whitbread records during the Cape Town stop-over by marrying a local girl within five days of meeting her. The couple met up again in Auckland and Burrel then set a second Whitbread first with the speed of his divorce. By all accounts he was a free man again at Mar del Plata – the third stop-over.

One week out of Cape Town a force nine gale left *Flyer*'s crew struggling, first with a broken boom, and later when the boat broached under poled-out headsails, with a badly damaged mast. Conny van Rietschoten, who was spending long periods on the wheel, suffered an attack of angina, the first signs of heart trouble. But with the weather deteriorating further, there was little chance for him to rest and the pressure led to the Dutch skipper having a heart attack. By now *Flyer* was seventy miles south of the Kerguelen Islands, and eleven days from the nearest port, Fremantle. The crew wanted to divert, and Julian Fuller, *Flyer*'s doctor, wanted advice from Trevor Agnew, a cardiologist on *Ceramco*. Van Rietschoten would allow neither. Explaining afterwards, he said: 'The first three days were the most critical. I would have died before they could have got me to port. Also, it was hard enough keeping ahead of *Ceramco* which was by then breathing down our necks just six miles astern. If they had known I had a health problem, the Kiwis would have pushed their boat even harder!'

Van Rietschoten lived to tell of the high stakes played out in the Southern Ocean. His yacht arrived in Auckland to an extraordinary welcome nine hours ahead of *Ceramco*, leaving Blake and his boys with the considerable kudos of winning their home leg on handicap.

Behind them the toll of damage continued to grow. *FCF Challenger* broke her backstay, boom and spinnaker poles while the crews from *33 Export*, *Licor 43* and *European University of Belgium* all faced up to the problems of being dismasted in the Southern Ocean. *Skopbank of Finland* and *Disque d'Or* suffered broken booms and *Save Venice* and *Swedish Entry* were both forced to pull out of the race once they had reached Auckland.

On the next stage to Cape Horn, *Flyer* and *Ceramco* enjoyed a classic duel to be first to Cape Horn similar to the tea-clipper rivalry between *Cutty Sark* and *Thermopylae* a century before. Both crews were convinced they had the faster boat, both were determined to be first at the Horn. The only difference between this and earlier clipper battles was that radios now made it possible for the world to follow the spectacle as it unfolded.

To the delight of all New Zealanders, *Ceramco* gained the initial advantage after taking a more southerly route from Auckland. Two hair-raising weeks followed as both crews pressed as much sail as they dared in conditions that rarely moderated below force six and were more often force eight. Conny van Rietschoten takes up the story:

'The day after hearing of *Ceramco*'s lead, we too picked up the strong westerlies, and running with the full-size 3oz spinnaker in force six to seven winds, covered 164 miles in twelve hours (an average of 13.7 knots) to reduce the Kiwi lead to seventeen miles. The next day was even better, 327 miles from noon to noon – *Flyer*'s best daily run – which set a new Whitbread record and pulled back a further twelve miles on the Farr design. *Flyer*'s speed indicator was rarely registering less than fifteen knots but, stung by our improving position, Blake and his boys obviously pressed their boat even harder, for the next day they regained twenty miles on us after our chicken chute (one smaller than a storm spinnaker) blew out.

The following day we notched up another 300 miles – four more than *Ceramco* – and the morning after *Flyer* broke into the lead. The first we knew of it was a radio call from Peter Blake soon after dawn. "We see you have your red, white and blue up this morning," he called over the VHF. "Look over your left shoulder and you might see us." One of us had to climb up to the first spreader on the mast before they were sighted less than a mile astern. It was an incredible coincidence, for we were exactly half way to the Horn, some 2,325 miles from the nearest land. How could two yachts be so close with all this desolate ocean to sail in?'

Yet they were to cross each other's tracks, within sight, three times more before *Flyer* finally reached the Horn less than five miles ahead of her rival, both beating the previous best time from Auckland set by Tabarly's *Pen Duick VI* four years before, by a two-and-a-half day margin.

Even then the race was not over. Soon after rounding up into the Atlantic, a shift in the wind handed *Ceramco* the lead. *Flyer*'s longer length helped wear the New Zealanders down on the predominantly windward leg north to Mar del Plata and the Dutch yacht eventually pulled out a seven-hour lead. The Kiwis, however, beat them on handicap again to win the prestigious Roaring Forties trophy for the best corrected time across the Southern Ocean legs.

Behind them, the fleet was cut through by a scythe of

***Flyer* under twin headsails in a Southern Ocean gale.**
Opposite: *Bubblegum*, Iain McGowan-Fyfe's Contessa 43, the 'baby' of the third race, which retired from leg three.

tion. *Gauloises III* had been dismasted just 1,300 miles out of Auckland leaving Loizeau with the uncertain consolation of retiring northwards to Tahiti. The same fate was to strike the Spanish yacht *Licor 43* for the second time during the race, but with the rig falling down just 100 miles west of the Horn, there was no holiday island to escape to. Instead, the crew were forced to set up a jury rig, and made it to Mar del Plata just in time to re-rig and join the fleet for the last stage.

Another who counted himself lucky to make it home was Paolo Martinoni, the Italian crewman washed overboard from *Rollygo*. The crew hurriedly doused the spinnaker and turned the yacht round, but soon lost sight of him in the darkness. Mercifully, they could hear him shouting and, guided back by his voice, threw him a lifebelt and light on their first pass. He was lucky. Water temperatures were down to six degrees centigrade, and once back on board he was found to be suffering badly from hypothermia.

Bubblegum's crew were left with a considerable problem to chew over after one of their number unscrewed the top retaining bolts in an effort to release a badly-sticking rudder shaft, only to have it fall through the bottom of the boat. To make matters worse, they were just 600 miles west of Cape Horn. All that Iain McGowan-Fyfe's team could do was to make up a jury rig by bolting two round metal discs to the end of a spinnaker pole and trail it over the stern as a sweep. They made remarkable progress, covering more than 100 miles a day towards Punta Arenas until meeting up with a Chilean tug.

Handicap honours on this leg went to Pierre Fehlmann's *Disque d'Or III* after she had enjoyed unusually swift running conditions all the way north from Cape Horn. Overall, Alain Gabbay and his crew on *Charles Heidsieck III* appeared to have a hold on the Whitbread trophy. By now they had built up a substantial handicap lead over their French champagne rivals on *Kriter IX*, despite breaking their boom, to leave *Flyer* trailing a poor third.

Remarkably, *Flyer* sailed the remaining miles back to Portsmouth without tacking to beat *Ceramco* (which tacked only once to clear England's south coast) by seventeen hours to clip fourteen days off *Great Britain II*'s record with a time of 120 days six hours. Despite their dismasting, Blake and his boys finished third on elapsed time and won the last leg on handicap – a performance in stark contrast to that of Blake's former skipper, Les Williams. His yacht *FCF Challenger* suffered breakages throughout and was finally dismasted 200 miles north east of the Azores, to finish the race sixth on elapsed time and sixteenth on handicap.

Luck also turned against *Charles Heidsieck*'s crew who ran slap into the Azores High. In a desperate attempt to lighten ship they threw their food and stores overboard, but failed to save their time, handing *Flyer*'s crew a unique handicap and elapsed time double, after dropping more than 140 hours in the calms.

K
1024

Cornelis van Rietschoten

When Cornelis van Rietschoten appeared on the Whitbread scene in 1977, few knew anything about him and fewer still rated his chances. The retired industrialist had not set foot on a racing yacht for more than thirteen years. How could this unsponsored Dutchman compete on equal terms against the experience of big names like Robin Knox-Johnston, Eric Tabarly or Rob James? But he showed everyone, beating the fleet into Cape Town and going on to win the race by almost sixty hours on handicap. Even then, few knew much about him, least of all his crew.

A private man, he says of his crew: 'There was no need for them to know about my personal life and I did not need to know about theirs – unless it affected the performance of the boat.'

After winning the principal handicap prize in 1978 with the 65ft Sparkman and Stephens-designed alloy ketch *Flyer*, he returned in 1981 aboard a Frers-designed maxi (also named *Flyer*) with the aim of winning the elapsed time record. He and his crew managed that with ease and, in a remarkable nail-biting finish, picked up the double after Alain Gabbay's French challenger *Charles Heidsieck* ran out of wind on the return leg.

Van Rietschoten ran both projects as a business and his boats on an employer/employee basis. He may well have been described as an amateur but he set new levels of professionalism within the sport that were not repeated until Peter Blake's victory in 1990.

He was accused by other crews and by one or two notable dissenters within his own number after these races, of running a draconian regime. 'I make no apologies. There is no room on a racing yacht for democracy. Someone has to be in charge. There has to be a clear chain of command and everyone needs to know exactly what they have to do and what is expected of them,' he says now. 'The system worked well and we won both races – and that's what matters.'

'The general rules I drew up would have come as second nature to experienced hands but, from my experience of running a large company, youngsters drawn from all walks of life need a common code to live by if team spirit is to work effectively in cramped, uncomfortable conditions over extended periods.'

His thirty-three-strong list of rules included a ban on talking about politics and complaints about the food. Each crewman was also given a specific job description which resolved arguments over duties.

The first to question his ability to lead a Whitbread campaign was Rod Stephens when van Rietschoten approached his Madison Avenue design firm to draw up the first *Flyer*. After listening to the Dutchman for an hour, Stephens averted his eyes and, with a voice filled with embarrassed undertones, questioned: 'Can you really handle this – you honestly think you can do a race like this?'

His answer was short and to the point and later, when Stephens saw the Dutchman's business plan for winning the race as well as his detailed rules and job descriptions for each crew, the American designer threw in a few points of his own. Following his first victory, Stephens gave this skipper the highest of accolades by paralleling his meticulous preparations to those of Harold Vanderbilt's during his masterful defence of the America's Cup in 1937 in the great J-class yacht *Ranger*.

Van Rietschoten began sailing at the age of three aboard his father's 12-Metre yacht. After the Second World War, he went to work and study in England, and invested a £200 football pools win into a friend's Dragon keelboat which the pair sailed first from the Clyde round to Newhaven on the English south coast, then across the North Sea to Norway to compete in the Dragon Gold Cup.

'It was a remarkable voyage, and I learned a lot about long distance sailing,' he recalls now. 'Our navigation was no great shakes and we lost our way several times, sailing well outside the safety of the 'swept' channels. We suffered so badly from loss of sleep and lack of food that both of us found ourselves hallucinating. It is a wonder now that we got there at all and were not blown up by a mine. The experience certainly gave me a good grounding on how not to tackle such an adventure in the future.'

During the 1950s van Rietschoten enjoyed a half-share in the Robert Clark-designed racing yawl *Maze*, competing in several Cowes Weeks and the 1957 Fastnet race during which the yacht was dismasted in a gale off Portland Bill.

Then tuberculosis seemingly put an end to his sailing career. He spent a year convalescing in a Swiss sanatorium, then threw all his remaining energies into running the family electrical engineering business until selling out at the age of forty-five.

Looking to find fresh interests, it was newspaper reports of the first Whitbread that first suggested a circumnavigation. 'My grandfather designed and built a yacht specifically to sail around the world, but left it too late in life to achieve this ambition. I was much younger, and plans for a second Whitbread lent more appeal to the idea, for I thought a race would satisfy both my competitive instincts as well as my sense for adventure,' he recalls.

Van Rietschoten's entry in the 1977/78 race was one of the first received by the organisers, but at the time he was still far

CORNELIS VAN RIETSCHOTEN

Conny van Rietschoten's *Flyer*, the first-leg leader into Cape Town, reaching away from Table Mountain at the start of the second leg in 1977/78.

from convinced that he was either fit or experienced enough to cope with the challenge.

'Thirteen years was a long time away from the sport. The technical advances had been enormous,' he admitted at the time. He began by drawing up a list of pros and cons and his confidence was given little encouragement when the minus column heavily outweighed any positive points he could muster.

'Initially, I had just four things going for me: I had been sailing all my life; had a strong competitive spirit; had been trained to manage people and projects, and could employ others to do the tasks I was unsure about.' He went away for a weekend to mull things over and by the end of it he had determined in his own mind how the campaign should be run.

It began by choosing the best designer and builder to improve on Ramon Carlin's race-winning formula in 1973. The Mexican's sixty-five-foot production yacht had proved the optimum size for winning handicap honours, so he called on Stephens to design a faster version. Aluminium was then thirty per cent lighter than glassfibre construction, so he turned to Wolter Huisman's specialist Dutch yard to build him a winner.

But it was his preparations before the race to turn himself and a crew into a race-winning team that impressed Stephens most, and ultimately distinguished van Rietschoten's efforts from the rest. While others like Robin Knox-Johnston and Les Williams were content just to get their yachts to the start-line in one piece, *Flyer* covered more than 10,000 miles of proving trials that included two transatlantic crossings and victory in that year's race from the US port of Manchester back to Plymouth. It resulted in several crew changes, more than one hundred alterations to the yacht and a team that was better prepared than any other when the cannon fired off Portsmouth that September. Van Rietschoten kept to the same formula in 1981, though changed designer to German Frers after seeing his maxi-yacht for Herbert von Karajan taking shape at Huisman's yard the previous year.

He also invested heavily in research to improve crew clothing, rigging and weather forecasting, areas that had been found wanting during the previous race, which all contributed to his crew clipping fourteen days off the record for the voyage.

But there is a lighter side to this Dutchman's steely and businesslike approach, and his crews enjoyed exploiting it. The common language onboard was English but, during the first race, van Rietschoten and his two Dutch watch-leaders, Jerry Dijkstra and Aedgard Koekebakker, often reverted to their native tongue when it came to discussing tactics or confidential issues. With one exception, the rest of the team never understood a word and, in mock rebuke, nicknamed the trio the 'Three Commissars' with Conny, Jerry and Aedgard known individually as Blockhead One, Two and Three. 'I never knew what they were talking about until long after the race,' van Rietschoten smiles now. 'I thought they were referring to buoys in the North Sea.'

H23
H 2398

Surfing in the Southern Ocean, *Flyer*'s helmsman enjoys the ultimate thrill. The speed would often touch 20 knots or more. Opposite: *Flyer*'s crew engaged in a regular day's work in the Southern Ocean.

Both *Flyers* were ostensibly 'dry' ships, but the Dutchman kept a stock of booze under his bunk to reward his team whenever they achieved a good day's run.

He lost control of it during the second race, however, after Koekebakker, who was van Rietschoten's project manager and right-hand man throughout the maxi campaign, overcame the liquor limitations by cutting a secret access hole through the bulkhead dividing his cabin from Conny's and by helping themselves to the beers within.

'We would put a hand through and pull out the beers whenever he was on watch or asleep, and cough to disguise the sound of opening them,' Koekebakker recalled with a wicked grin. 'The one problem was the fact that we were always taking cans from the bottom and one day the whole pile crashed down while Conny was in his bunk asleep. We thought it was the end, but luckily he was so tired, the noise failed to wake him.'

Boys will always be boys; Koekebakker particularly, who coated his skipper with ice-cream during victory celebrations after both races. Laughing, van Rietschoten turned to his friends after receiving the second baptism, saying: 'Now, you can realise why I have to be so tough on them when we are at sea!'

While he enjoyed the parties ashore, there was no disguising the Dutchman's determination afloat. The best example was when he suffered a heart attack in the Southern Ocean during the 1981/82 race. It was a particularly stressful time. The winds were storm force. His yacht had suffered several bad knockdowns, her boom had broken and the mast had been damaged. Worse, Peter Blake's *Ceramco New Zealand* was pressing hard for the lead.

His crew wanted to head towards Fremantle, Australia, the nearest port and Julian Fuller, the doctor onboard, wanted desperately to discuss treatment with the cardiologist racing on *Ceramco*. Van Rietschoten would hear of neither. 'Fremantle was ten days sailing away. If I was to die the critical period was within the first two to three days, so any diversion would have been wasted. As for *Ceramco*, the New Zealanders were already breathing down our necks. If they had known I had a health problem, they would have pushed their boat even harder. We had to stay ahead and the less they knew about my condition the better.

'When you die at sea, you are buried over the side. Perhaps those *Ceramco* boys might have spotted me drifting by, and I was determined that that would be the only thing they would see or hear from *Flyer* on that matter!' he told people later.

Thanks to Fuller's care, van Rietschoten recovered, *Flyer* beat *Ceramco* into Auckland by nine hours and went on to win what became known as 'The Dutch Double' – line and handicap honours; a feat not repeated until Peter Blake won at his fifth attempt in 1990.

Chapter Four

The 1985·86 Race

***Drum*, in Falmouth after losing her keel in the 1985 Fastnet six weeks prior to the Whitbread start. Opposite: *Drum*, salvaged and repaired, made the start of the 1985/86 race.**

The fourth running of the Whitbread over the northern winter of 1985/86 was dubbed 'the light one' by the crews that returned. But what it lacked in weather was more than compensated for by the intense competition within the sixteen-strong fleet. They seemed to face just as many problems too. Dismastings put paid to the chances of two yachts, structural problems plagued two more, and one lost its rudder after colliding with a whale.

Back for a fourth 'bite of the cherry' was Peter Blake with a design far removed from *Ceramco*. One of seven maxi-sized yachts to challenge for line honours, his Ron Holland-designed 78ft *Lion New Zealand* was not only the heaviest yacht in the fleet, but carried a record number of crew – twenty-two – Blake's theory being that *Flyer* could have been pushed much harder last time round with a 'round-the-buoys' crew.

In contrast Pierre Fehlmann was one of three skippers to develop Bruce Farr's *Ceramco* design concept for this, his third crack at the race. With backing from a Swiss bank, he surrounded himself with the best in the business to build and campaign the 80ft *UBS Switzerland*. The result was a composite maxi weighing 61,140lb (28,000kg), some 4,500lb lighter than any of her rivals and 15,500lb less than *Lion NZ*! The finished hull was flown from her yard in Geneva to Monte Carlo in a Super-Guppy transporter where his eighteen crew began a series of extensive trials that were to take them across the Atlantic and back, compete in two round-the-buoys maxi events, as well as the Fastnet before taking on the Big Event.

Blake was in a similar state of preparation. Like *Ceramco*, his latest yacht had conquered the demanding Sydney/Hobart race before being shipped to America and sailing across the Atlantic. Many of his crew were veterans of the previous campaign and the boat was ready a full week before the start – and her rivals.

The notable latecomers were Eric Tabarly's 83ft Belgian

K-3797
DRUM

UBS, Pierre Fehlmann's Farr-designed maxi rater, line honours winner of the fourth race.

Grand old man of the sea Eric Tabarly aboard the Belgian entry *Cote d'Or*. Opposite: Lionel Péan's *L'Esprit d'Equipe*, handicap winner of the fourth race.

entry *Cote d'Or* and *Drum*, a sistership to *Lion NZ* owned by Simon Le Bon, the lead singer from the pop group Duran Duran. The latter had been commissioned for Rob James who had tragically drowned the previous year. Le Bon and his two business partners, Paul and Michael Berrow, had bought the boat in an unfinished state and installed Skip Novak as their project manager and skipper.

They could not have chosen a better man for the job. He proved himself an expert in crisis management. The first drama came when *Drum*'s keel fell off and the boat capsized, shortly after the start of the Fastnet race. Those crew, trapped below decks in the upturned hull, were lucky to survive. Some were pinned down by the weight of sails while others choked on the fumes from spilt battery acid and diesel fuel floating inside. All were thankful that the accident happened within sight of shore and the alert so immediate that an RAF rescue helicopter was hovering overhead within minutes.

Lesser skippers and owners would have called it a day there and then but Novak, once given the go-ahead, rallied his team to achieve the impossible – completely re-fitting and re-rigging their yacht in the six weeks that remained before the start. They did it, just, but their troubles were far from over.

Tabarly's problems were even more fundamental. Sponsorship had been late to materialise and his Joubert/Nivelt design had to be built in an unholy five-month rush. The Brussels-based chocolate manufacturer which underwrote all the costs of the campaign originally wanted an all-Belgian crew but, with no time to tune the boat or train a team, she eventually carried ten French professionals and, with the exception of Luc Heymans, Tabarly's second-in-command, seven 'amateur' Belgians. Launched less than two months before the start, the yacht turned out four tons heavier than her designed displacement and after the Fastnet race, her only proving trial, the crew set out on the Whitbread having not had time to hoist half their sail wardrobe or test the boat downwind in strong conditions.

Before the start *Atlantic Privateer*, the Farr-designed eighty-footer built in South Africa by Padda Kuttel, looked to be the strongest challenger. Her crew had shown the fastest pace in the Seahorse Maxi series that preceded the Whitbread and her crew were experienced. The one doubt was their mast, bought second-hand as a training rig from *Flyer*. The mast and much of its standing rigging had already taken the Dutch maxi to victory four years earlier and, with 40,000 hard racing miles to its credit, many judged it too tired to complete another circumnavigation. They were to be proved right.

Completing the line-up of maxis was Digby Taylor's low-budget challenge aboard another Farr maxi, *NZI Enterprise*, together with the venerable *Great Britain II*, now in the hands of Bob Salmon, which underwent an eve of race name change to *Norsk Data GB*.

Within the list of challengers for handicap honours the hottest names were Dirk Nauta, Lionel Péan from France and the Spanish designer/skipper Javier Visiers. Nauta, the dour Dutchman whose cruiser/racer *Tielsa* completed the second Whitbread, returned with the purpose-built Judel/Vrolijk-designed 63ft *Philips Innovator*. Visiers had designed the 62ft composite-built *Fortuna Lights* which proved fast 'right out of the box', winning the Spanish Route of Discovery transatlantic race immediately after her launching.

By contrast Péan had chosen a boat built for the previous race. His 58ft *L'Esprit d'Equipe* was the former *33 Export*, a lightweight Briand design that had shown great promise until losing her mast off the Kerguelen Islands in the Indian Ocean. The twenty-seven-year-old from St Malo called on the French designer to up-date the alloy yacht and, after spending three months in a shipyard, she emerged with a re-modelled stern, a new keel adding two tons to displacement and a taller fractional rig. Péan and his crew suffered a shroud failure during their first major trial, the Route of Discovery race, but went on to beat all their Whitbread rivals in the Florida-based SORC circuit. By the Fastnet race, six weeks before the start of the Whitbread, both crew and boat were in a high state of preparation, proving this by finishing second among the Whitbread contenders behind *Atlantic Privateer*.

Others in the line-up included a second Dutch entry, Pleun van der Lugt's Baltic 55 *Equity & Law*, two Swan production yachts, the Frers-designed 651 *Fazer Finland*, built for Michael Berner, and the 51ft *Shadow of Switzerland* entered by the husband and wife team Otto and Nora Zehender-Mueller. Completing the list was Gustaaf Versluys' Guy Ribadeau Dumas-designed *Rucanor Tristar* from Belgium and the Danish cruiser *SAS Baia Viking*, skippered by Jesper Norsk.

F. 8333
F. 8333
l'esprit d'équipe

During the first leg to Cape Town Péan and his crew enjoyed a fair measure of luck, first sailing through the Doldrums without pause, then avoiding a storm off the Cape of Good Hope which destroyed so many hopes.

At Cape Town, once again, repairs were needed to rectify the second 'demolition derby' in succession. If the 1981/82 race had had more than its fair share of destruction of yachts on the first leg, this one had an excess. *Atlantic Privateer* had been dismasted – twice if you count the 'water-pipe' mast erected at Luderitz – *NZI Enterprise* had a bend in hers which rendered it totally useless. Two other maxis, *Drum* and *Cote d'Or*, needed major constructional repairs after being in serious danger of breaking up – only two other maxis, *UBS Switzerland* and *Lion New Zealand* survived relatively unscathed.

Padda Kuttel had tried hard to keep *Atlantic Privateer* racing after the hard driving of watch-captain David Bongers had resulted in the mast falling down. Bongers had certainly put the boat into a winning position but at an unpayable price. The idea of a 'Heath Robinson' mast, made from waterpipes, came from within the crew but even their ingenuity was not enough to make it work and they had already disqualified themselves from the leg by motoring to Luderitz. Bongers left the crew as soon as *Atlantic Privateer* arrived at his home port of Cape Town. *NZI Enterprise* had a new mast air-freighted from New Zealand to Cape Town which arrived before the boat.

Drum also had serious problems to repair. There had been rush enough to get the boat ready after her Fastnet capsize but this time she needed major surgery and a constructional rebuild as the hull had delaminated and the floor was flexing through the strains imposed by the keel. Adrian Thompson, who had engineered her construction, and Butch Dalrymple-Smith of the Ron Holland Design office, flew in to investigate what might be done and agreed that, within the time scale, she might just be repaired. It needed, however, round-the-clock working by the crew to complete the job with two days to spare. Eric Tabarly had similar, although not quite as comprehensive, repairs to make to *Cote d'Or*. In addition, concerned by the boat's bow-down propensity, he replaced the keel with a bulbed one which shifted the centre of balance further aft.

Péan's smaller French yacht arrived at the 'Tavern of the Seas' with nothing more than flaked paintwork to take an eleven-hour lead over *Philips Innovator*. But luck turns full circle during a race of this length, however, and during the closing stages of the next leg to Auckland the gods conspired to leave *L'Esprit d'Equipe* becalmed for two days on the run south down the east coast of New Zealand's North Island, which handed a grateful *Philips Innovator* crew a twelve-hour advantage on corrected time at this half-way stage.

It was during this stop-over that Péan and his crew found that their mast had bent at deck level. The same thing had also happened to *Cote d'Or*'s spar, but the French manufacturer responsible for both rigs, chose only to bolt two alloy sleeves over the damaged area, rather than go to the expense of flying out new lower sections.

Setting out on the third leg in mid February, *L'Esprit d'Equipe* soon began to claw back the Dutch advantage. Eleven days out into the ice-strewn South Atlantic, however, Péan reported to race control that the mast had split in two just below the deck while they were enjoying rare surfing conditions enroute to Cape Horn. The crew saved the day by bolting spare boom sleeves over the damaged area, then setting up a series of Spanish windlasses above and below deck to support the repair.

Much to Nauta's consternation, the French yacht hardly missed a beat, continuing at her previous fast pace, losing only sixty miles while the repairs were made. By the time the fleet arrived at Punta del Este, the new Uruguayan stop-over, *L'Esprit's* ecstatic crew had not only recaptured the overall lead, but built up a five-hour advantage over *Philips Innovator* for the final tactical leg back to Portsmouth. The deficit left Nauta a beaten man – '*L'Esprit* is a very fast boat upwind and the crew will be extremely difficult to beat now,' the Dutch skipper prophesied.

He was right. Equipped with a new lower section of mast, belatedly shipped in by *L'Esprit d'Equipe*'s spar manufacturer, Péan and his crew soon headed the handicap listings on this 6,300-mile leg back to Portsmouth, leaving Nauta wallowing back in ninth place. Once past the Azores High, the strong south westerly air-stream, enjoyed by all the fleet, helped *Philips Innovator* pull back some lost ground but, unable to overtake *L'Esprit*'s time, her crew had to rest content with second place overall, finishing twenty-two hours behind the victorious Whitbread trophy winner, Lionel Péan.

The race for line honours developed into a 'tortoise and hare' event. As predicted, the first to falter was *Atlantic Privateer* though, ironically, her dismasting was caused by the collapse of a new diagonal shroud fitted just prior to the start which failed at the tang. Robbed of all chance to win line honours, skipper Padda Kuttel's priorities changed to being first into each succeeding port – a feat achieved with just seven minutes to spare at Auckland after an exciting duel with Taylor's *NZI Enterprise* over the final 200 miles south from Cape Reinga.

Cote d'Or's downfall came while challenging *Atlantic Privateer* for the lead during the Cape storm, 200 miles from the finish of the first leg. The composite-structured yacht suffered substantial core failure over a wide area of the port bow after slamming into head seas for more than four days. Her crew, fearful that the panting hull might cave in at any point, spent a nerve-wracking two days riding out the storm on port tack before limping into harbour with her bows shored up with poles and flooring. This was followed by a hectic month of repairs and modifications which included the fitting of a new keel to overcome the yacht's dangerous bow-down trim. This had caused some frightening submarine dives during the first stage; a change that brought with it a ninety-eight hour penalty on the yacht's overall time, imposed by the race committee.

This was not the end of their delamination problems. During the second stage to Auckland, a rogue strip of adhesive tape left in place during the yacht's lay-up resulted in further failure, this time in the forefoot area.

The damage was discovered by Luc Heymans during a private moment sitting on a bucket in the forepeak. 'I had my hands on the floor to balance myself and suddenly felt the hull moving up and down beneath me,' he said. The realisation that the hull could split at any moment and that he might be caught squatting below the waterline proved a sure cure for

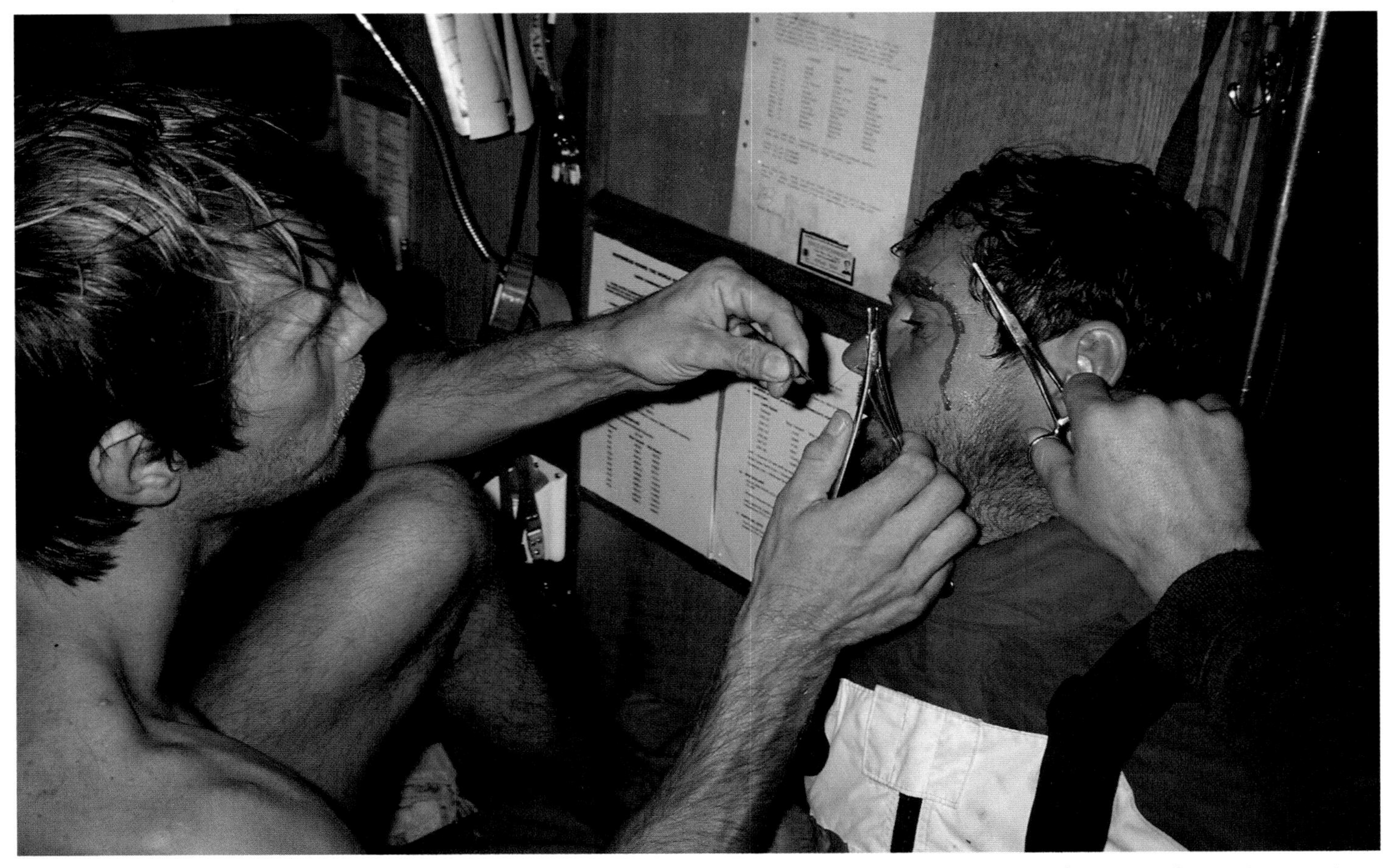

Doctor Roger Nilson stitches fellow *Drum* crew member's wounds. Below: *Drum* and *Cote d'Or* ashore for major repairs in Cape Town. Both had severe delamination problems which caused their crews a great deal of anxiety on leg one.

Idyllic sailing conditions for *Drum*'s crew. Opposite: the full extent of the damage to *NZI Enterprise*'s mast at the end of leg one was only revealed when the yacht docked in Cape Town.

constipation and Heymans rushed on deck to tell the bad news.

Unsure of the extent of the problem, Tabarly had no option but to head north into warmer waters in case the hull split open, losing further time. From Auckland onwards, however, *Cote d'Or* and her crew began to show their potential, finishing a close second to Fehlmann's *UBS Switzerland* both at Punta del Este and the finish.

Like *Cote d'Or*, the similar structural failure suffered by Simon Le Bon's crew on *Drum* seriously handicapped their performance though, once repairs to her hull and keel had been made in Cape Town, the yacht moved steadily up the fleet to finish third on elapsed time.

Structural problems also beset *NZI Enterprise* though her eventual Achilles heel proved to be her fractional mast. First the top of the mast collapsed during the same storm off Cape Town that crippled so many others, then the replacement spar also crashed down off Chatham Island during the early stages of the third leg, forcing her retirement.

In contrast, Peter Blake's *Lion New Zealand* proved to be one of the strongest yachts in the fleet but, being also the heaviest, she did not have the pace to compete against her larger rivals. Withstanding everything that came her way, except a whale that broke her rudder in the Tasman, she would have been beaten by a two-minute margin into second place by *Cote d'Or* had the race committee not imposed a time penalty for fitting a new keel during the Cape Town stop-over. This dropped Tabarly's red yacht back to fourth overall.

Instead, the honours and much of the publicity fell on Pierre Fehlmann's *UBS Switzerland* which set a twenty-four-hour record of 374 miles and a new time of 117 days, fourteen-and-a-half hours, which was more than two days inside *Flyer*'s previous best performance.

Tabarly's *Cote d'Or* reaching fast.

Profile

Lionel Péan

Beautiful and difficult is how Lionel Péan described the Whitbread. Those two attributes provided the fascination for what, in his estimation, remains the ultimate race. They were a constant goad; indeed, had been for many years. It was simply putting all the logistics in place that enabled Péan, a married man with one child, to attempt his personal goal. 'My decision to race was based more on emotion than on career tactics,' he admitted.

For years he had been putting the parts together, rather like a jigsaw, gaining experience wherever he went, obtaining the results that are so necessary to attract commercial sponsorship and, as much as anything, finding the right companions.

Sailing had always been part of his life, yet the early years were not ones filled with ambition; that was to come later. He started, like almost everyone, in a family dinghy, one built by his father, which he sailed off La Rochelle. The family influence continued to develop his sailing and included a sabbatical cruise to Brazil. For the adolescent Péan, this seemed dull; he needed the cutting edge of competition for stimulation. Before he was sixteen he had crossed the Atlantic again, sailing to the Caribbean on *Striano*. It was an adventure which allowed him to consider his future, a time to dream with objectivity.

He discovered the buzz of racing with Philippe Briand and quickly accepted its narcotic-like addiction. There were never enough races, never enough days afloat. He tried them all, the more important they were, the more he liked them; the more impossible, the greater his urge to compete. With Briand, he found the entrée to the world of the Ton Cups, the Admiral's Cup, Olympic racing in Solings; there was simply nothing he didn't want to try.

Then came the deep-sea adventure races, the single-handed challenges that are so much a part of the way of life of a French ocean racer. They are very much part of the public domain and a shop window for the ambitious sailor. Péan was fully aware of that and when he didn't win he was publicly analytical of his failure. He raced the French mini-transat and admitted that he didn't have what it took to win. 'I lost and I took that loss hard,' he said. When he thought he had found a good boat for the Figaro, the half-ton single-handed race of four legs, he failed to win and said, 'I should have given the sponsor his money back.'

He continued along the traditional route in France, racing with and against the top names in that country in international events whenever he could. He is a dynamo of a man, constantly charging his batteries and those of all around him. He raced with Mike Birch and Florence Arthaud; he made friends with Daniel Gilard and all the time he made it patently obvious that he was going places and that his dreams would be realised.

The principle dream was the Whitbread. He had sown the seed in his mind as he sailed across the Atlantic when only fifteen. It might have been a child's dream, but it was one to which he held with fervour and passion. He needed a team and chose one which put a premium on efficiency rather than friendship, yet the band of faithful fanatics were the men who were to find their place aboard *L'Esprit d'Equipe*, many of whom he wouldn't have hesitated to have called friend.

Péan's philosophy, of building a team around which he could concentrate his efforts to win the Whitbread, was fully appreciated by Group Bull, a communications and computer company of 26,000 employees, who decided to sponsor the challenge. True to the philosophy, they did not demand their name to be on the boat; they too wished to be part of the team. Jacques Stern, chairman of Bull, said of them: 'The eight-man crew, the symbol of our firm, set out dreaming of victory . . . '

The managing director of Bull, Francis Lorentz, went further in his analogy of Péan and his crew with the sponsoring company. 'Like a boat, the success of a company relies on the individual abilities of the men and the women it employs, as well as on their collective efficiency in action and their will to work together to win.' He added: 'It was to illustrate these beliefs that Bull entered a boat and crew in the 1985/86 Round the World Race choosing the name *L'Esprit d'Equipe*: team spirit. Rather than promote its name, Bull, along with Lionel Péan and his crew, chose to highlight a certain philosophy instead.

Péan was twenty-nine when he entered the Whitbread arena. Rather than take a new boat, he decided to modify one which had been built for the previous race, a fifty-eight-footer designed by his friend, Philippe Briand, which raced under the name of *33 Export* and retired after being dismasted in the Southern Ocean on leg two. One year before the start Péan began his modifications to the design changes wrought by Briand. The main alterations to the hull were to the stern shape, to make the boat more powerful when reaching. Just over six feet was added to the height of the rig and, to compensate for this, more lead was added to the keel which, in its turn, was moved further aft. Each change brought greater efficiency and Péan was at the centre of all those changes; he was totally involved in every opportunity to make improvements; improvements that would give him a better chance to win.

The partnership within and around the boat were the driving forces for Péan. Each time he enhanced them, the pressure built on him, but for Péan, this was the stimulus he sought. He

Race-winner Lionel Péan and the crew of *L'Esprit d'Equipe* display Gallic team spirit in their celebrations at the end of the race in Gosport.

needed to be driven hard and, in turn, drives hard. 'Not everyone considers me a friend,' he says. 'I know how to push my weight around and like to say what I think.' He is cautious about making friends, but once made, they remain friends for ever.

'On board, I show the men I have confidence. I try to be on everybody's back. I decided to be off watch and play the big boss. That way I can judge situations objectively and cut down any risk of error.' Péan is a hard task-master; one who pushes his crew to the limit, but is prepared, at the same time, to give of his own all. 'Although I'm tolerant of people in everyday living, I won't put up with technical mistakes. There is only one goal: to win!'

The dedicated Péan had his detractors, but there were none at the end of the race who could deny him the well-deserved victory. He had, in his own admission, set his sights high, but it is the measure of the man that he was able to maintain his aim in a way that few others could ever hope to do. There are only going to be a few Whitbread winners and while the race was raced on handicap, there were many variables. Péan had to make choices; choices that were restricted by budget; and he chose wisely.

The boat was in the right rating band; the crew were magnificent and were reinforced for the two Southern Ocean legs. Yvan Griboval sailed from Cape Town to Auckland and Péan encouraged his friend Daniel Gilard to go round Cape Horn. Péan's comments on adding to his close-knit crew provide an insight to the man. 'Yvan, and then Daniel, did it, each in his own way. Two different personalities and two difference experiences. Their arrival amplified my role as co-ordinator to restore a balance between forces that had changed. I think there is only one way to fit in, and that's to blend in with the group without trying to impose your own way. To be modest.'

Péan will always be remembered for his modesty and for his leadership. The latter shows through in his comment about the setting of boundaries of privacy in the community of the crew. 'You have to be competent and solid to do that. That was one of my guidelines in choosing my crew, each man having a technological speciality. Concerning the boundaries between them and me, my role consisted of taking long-term options at the chart table and regulating the boat's progress. The watch on deck was totally responsible for short-term considerations in order to get the most out of the boat at any given moment.' His ability to delegate responsibility, the true test of management, was the ultimate weapon in his armoury for the Whitbread.

Lionel Péan won the fourth Whitbread by almost a day on corrected time. He said he was really relaxed as soon as *L'Esprit d'Equipe* sailed into the English Channel, knowing that only a disaster could rob them of their win. For him, the best moment of the race was the night when he saw both Cape Horn and Halley's Comet; and the worst was when they sailed the last two hundred miles into Auckland 'without so much as a breath of wind.'

Profile

Pierre Fehlmann

Pierre Fehlmann is an easy man to find. Stroll along any Whitbread Race dock and look for a man with a briefcase under his arm and a purposeful stride and it is bound to be Fehlmann. The Swiss skipper is the true professional; the Whitbread is his career. He moves from one race to another and missed only the first one in 1973. Pierre Fehlmann is fully occupied.

He is passionately in love with the Whitbread; he treats it as the great romance, an affair which soars beyond bliss and pleasure, one with sorrows that plummet to the depths. He was seduced by the race when he saw what happened in the first and has been its lover ever since. It is a compelling affair which drives him to permanent distraction with the need to fuel its wants.

Initially, a Swan 65 ketch, the sistership to *Sayula II*, the winner of the first race, was good enough for Fehlmann. Others were looking the same way and Pierre had the competitive edge, one honed in small dinghies. He felt that with a level playing field, he could hold sway.

Pierre Fehlmann's *UBS* on her way from Central Switzerland, where she was built, to the sea. She finished fourth.

He claims that he first went sailing while still in his mother's womb, aboard his father's boat on Lake Geneva, and he was certainly sailing there as a five-year-old, allegedly lashed to the mast of the family racing boat. It was there that he learned that racing is better than sailing and coming first is better than simply competing. The spark of being faster, being better, was ignited on waters far removed from those on which he was to make his name.

Fehlmann had the opportunities given to him, the son of a middle-class family to whom sailing was part of its way of life. Pierre was to make it his total way of life. He competed in Snipes as well as keelboats and then raced in the Vaurien class, being runner-up in European and world championships before moving to the 505s, where again he finished second in a European championship. It was the hard graft for obtaining recognition.

Fehlmann is a methodical man who appreciates the logical route to success. His early attempts to become part of the yachting establishment in his own country included a period of voluntary work in yachting administration, culminating in membership of the IYRU Youth Committee. He had, by then, already been the Swiss coach at the 1972 Olympics in Kiel and raced against the world's best.

But Fehlmann saw that there were other, less prosaic, goals to achieve. He wanted to free himself of the shackles of a bourgeois society and carve his own niche on the world's oceans. There were, he felt, greater challenges there and bigger rewards to go with them. He started in the blue water races by trying to win the Single-handed Transatlantic Race and came to grief when his boat sank under him.

Fehlmann was undeterred by the experience but he did realise that there was perhaps only the one opportunity to make a major mistake at sea, and get away with it, not only physically but in the eye of the public. It is important too not to repeat it for commercial reasons. The sponsors, while willing to accept the publicity a disaster brings, prefer their name to be connected with a success; preferably a string of successes.

He was fully aware of the measures by which a sports sponsorship is judged. Trained as an engineer – Fehlmann was later a sales manager for IBM – he knew the barriers which existed elsewhere in the sport had to be trampled down if there was to be any real purpose behind the funding. Yachting sponsorship was in its infancy and the administrators of the sport were giving major opportunities away for virtually nothing. For Fehlmann there had to be the chance to turn this into business, and a profit making one at that.

Where he had the advantage was that, coming from Switzerland, he had never had the restrictive constraints imposed upon him that the jealousies and envies found in the long-established yacht clubs do on others. He could begin a search for money for his campaigns without any restrictions whatsoever, even those

PIERRE FEHLMANN

UBS **arriving in Cape Town to be the first to finish in the 1985/86 race.**

Z-3333
Z-3333
763

which might elsewhere be seen as moral issues. Fehlmann knew that the way to success in sailboat racing lay in having a sound financial structure on which to base a campaign and he wasn't to be told by others where, or more precisely, where not to look.

To that end, he formed with other members of his family and friends the SORC, Swiss Ocean Racing Club, which was a vehicle for him to obtain commercial funding. It was a club which appeared to be part of the establishment but had none of the ties that would stifle its operation. For Fehlmann it was the ideal machine which would convert dreams into realities.

He tackled the tobacco companies as they had considerable funds available for promotional purposes but constantly reduced opportunities to utilise their money. Fehlmann was forthright; he wanted money, they needed publicity. Disque d'Or provided him with the funding for the Single-handed Transatlantic Race and stayed with him for the 1977/78 Whitbread and the Swan 65 bore their name. A fourth in that race was a well-achieved result. There were four boats from that mould in the race and only Nick Ratcliffe's *King's Legend*, the only cutter, could beat Fehlmann home.

The lessons of his first Whitbread were the basis of his campaign for the next. It had to be even more properly funded and those funds had to be committed early enough that the boat could be designed and built with time to sail her and discover any idiosyncrasies. The boat must have miles under its keel so that the crew would know and understand how to make the most of her and to eliminate any failings she might have. Fehlmann had the backing of the same tobacco company and, once again, he was to promote their brand, Disque d'Or.

Bruce Farr was his choice of naval architect; his level rating boats had been making major headlines and Fehlmann believed that Farr and aluminium could do for him what Sparkman & Stephens and the same material had done for Conny van Rietschoten in the previous race.

The boat was 'over-built' and came, unfortunately, overweight. For the Farr design, this was a disaster, but, strangely, Fehlmann seemed unaware of just how much difference an extra couple of tons was likely to make. Once more he finished fourth on handicap which set the Swiss skipper in an even more determined mood for the next race.

UBS Switzerland, to give her her full title, was an 80ft Bruce Farr design built of modern composites by Decision SA in Switzerland. The fractional rigged maxi had a displacement of 27.5 tons; she was Fehlmann's idea of what was needed to win the race, certainly to satisfy his banking sponsors and his other financial supporters by finishing first into the stop-over ports. Fehlmann had, at last, his 'rocket-ship' and he soon showed that he knew how to use it.

On the third day of the 1985/86 race, Fehlmann made the decision to tack out to the west and away from the light winds that the fleet were experiencing. He sailed that way for more than twelve hours into continuously increasing breezes and was into twenty knots before making the tack south. It was a devastating move that put *UBS* comfortably in front to go through the north-east trades and into the Doldrums. 'We based our strategy on a computer study of the weather patterns for the past four years,'

The celebrations begin for Pierre Fehlmann in Portsmouth. Opposite: *Disque d'Or*, a Swan 65 ketch, was Fehlmann's first Whitbread race entry.

said Fehlmann, safely moored in Duncan Dock at Cape Town after finishing more than sixteen hours ahead of the fleet. He had beaten Conny van Rietschoten's record for the leg by two days nine hours.

UBS didn't win the second leg, she was merely third and there was a great deal more determination about Fehlmann's effort for the third. That determination shows in the log after *UBS* had clocked 302.7 miles in twenty-four hours . . . 'We are crazy. Eighteen to twenty knots with flanker, close to broaching, just under the boat's safety limit. But we don't know what the safety limit is!' Fehlmann was not proposing to find out, he wanted to win. But he hadn't lost his sense of humour.

After the Le Maire Strait, with the rigours of the Southern Ocean behind, there was another record in *UBS*'s log: 'Pierre on deck!' The skipper explained it on the next line: 'Management by exception'. *UBS* went on to win that leg and the next and break the race record by two days sixteen hours.

Fehlmann had made his point but he also showed his sponsors value for money as *UBS* raced up the Solent from the Needles. He made four spinnaker changes so that the accompanying photographers could obtain a shot of each. Not only that, the sponsors were there in a boat to greet *UBS* and he knew that he might need them again in four years' time and there was no harm in showing his appreciation.

He was there for the next race and will be for the sixth. By dismissing the ketch option, which Farr had offered, he spoiled his own chances of winning. He did, however, learn his lesson and *Merit* was rigged as a ketch soon after the race in order that Fehlmann could test the twin-mast configuration for himself. In common with all the new maxis built for the 1993 race, his new boat has two masts. The sistership to the new *La Poste*, in other words, will be a ketch.

Part Two

The Last Race

IR-1992
IR
1992
JAMESON WHISKEY
ESB INTERNATIONAL
20

Chapter Five

The 1989 · 90 Race

On 2 September 1989 twenty-three boats on starboard tack charged at the starting line in twelve knots of breeze. The conditions were near-ideal in the Solent as the fifth Whitbread race got under way. Around them was the biggest spectator fleet ever assembled for a yacht race in the UK – more than four thousand boats of all sizes from outboard runabouts to cross-Channel ferries loaded with an estimated 50,000 people eager to see the fleet away on its 33,000-mile adventure.

Previous spread: *Steinlager 2* leads the fleet down the Solent. Above: *Fazisi*. Opposite: *NCB Ireland*.

Thankfully, it was an incident-free start with the spectators keeping well clear of the competitors as the leaders went away at well over ten knots. The sight was one of churned water – the Solent almost completely white with the wakes of the huge armada after the boats had been started, off the entrance to Southampton Water, by the Duke and Duchess of York aboard the frigate HMS *Ambuscade*. It was, arguably, as competitive a start as there has ever been in the history of the Whitbread, not one of the twenty-three skippers wishing to give even a second away and they were tightly packed toward the windward end of the line, five miles to the east of Cowes, heading for Hurst Narrows and the Needles, the last landmarks until Ushant on the first leg to Punta del Este in Uruguay 5,938 miles away.

NCB Ireland skippered by Joe English, had the pole position, fighting it out with *Fazisi*, the Russian boat which three days earlier had looked unlikely to start because of measurement problems. It was only round-the-clock work with British designer Tony Castro's invaluable input, which culminated in the boat being cleared to race only twenty-four hours before the off.

Before long, before they reached Cowes even, it was the two New Zealand ketches, *Steinlager 2* and *Fisher & Paykel*, that had begun to spearhead the fleet. The rivalry between those two was already on its way to legendary proportions – they finished just over two minutes apart in the Fastnet race – and it promised to be the highlight of the fifth Whitbread. *Steinlager 2*'s skipper, Peter Blake, dismissed the Fastnet win as having little relevance. But it provided him with a hands-on opportunity of real-time racing against the man and boat he acknowledged to be the one he feared the most, Grant Dalton in *Fisher & Paykel*, and it provided the technological boost in the sail wardrobe of the big red ketch.

Steinlager 2, with a completely new wardrobe of sails, led the cavalry charge down the Solent in a demonstration of sailing power. The New Zealand ketch was ahead before Blake called for a mizzen staysail to be set – the extra sail area developing more horsepower to take him further out in front. Behind him, Dalton was keeping his powder dry, doing enough, however, to keep the pack at bay.

In the three-and-a-half years since the finish of the last race, much had happened to the philosophy surrounding the race. The decision had been made that the maxis would race on level terms, without handicap, a foretaste of what might be likely in future races. This had attracted fifteen yachts into the major class with two more elderly maxis racing in a cruiser division. The others were grouped into three classes, one of them having a single entry. The writing, against handicap racing, was on the wall in large enough letters for all to see and take notice.

One designer in particular had examined the ketch rig in the IOR, the measurement rule under which the race is run, and had found a loophole which he suspected would give considerable advantage to the two-masted boats taking part this time. Bruce Farr had analysed the weather conditions which had been predicted for all six legs and reasoned that there would be adequate opportunity for a ketch to set the extra sail from the mizzen which would provide it with a greater chance of success.

Farr was undoubtedly one step ahead of his fellow designers but he was not totally persuasive with this clients. Pierre Fehlmann, who had raced in three previous Whitbreads, rejected the ketch option saying that he could not believe that it would be

***Merit*, Pierre Fehlmann's Farr-designed maxi sloop. Opposite: *Fisher & Paykel*, Grant Dalton's Farr-designed maxi ketch which pushed her compatriot so hard for so long, but never quite managed to match her.**

better from the experience he had gained when sailing a Swan 65 with a ketch rig in the 1977/78 race. His *Merit*, therefore, was sloop-rigged while the other three new Farr maxis all sported two masts. Dalton was the first to announce that he had decided on a ketch rig, with a masterly piece of public timing, to beat the others to the draw, but, like Roger Nilson, whose boat had originally been commissioned by Skip Novak, Dalton chose a masthead foretriangle.

Blake, who had had to scrap the first *Steinlager* hull when it failed to cure properly during construction, had some time to re-think the way his boat should be rigged. After much discussion with Farr, Blake chose a fractional rig, gaining with it more working sail area, although losing a small amount in the size of spinnakers. It was to prove a crucial choice.

For a southern hemisphere yacht, *Steinlager 2* was relatively late in the water, launching a week before Christmas 1988. Blake was not deterred by this; much of his preparation had been in the design stage and his phenomenal race experience gave him an advantage which none of his rivals could match. He had the biggest, longest waterlined boat in the fleet, fully aware that in a race where there was considerable reaching, he would have a distinct advantage. He had the latest design to come out of the Farr office and his 84ft ketch lacked nothing from her New Zealand brewery sponsor. Blake and his navigator, Mike Quilter, had already given the brewery value for money by winning the bicentennial round Australia race with the 60ft trimaran, *Steinlager 1*. Many of the fourteen on board with him had one or more Whitbreads under their belt and Blake had raced in every one. 'Big Red', as the boat became known to her crew, was everything that a skipper could possibly ask of his designer and builder.

From their arrival in England, the attitude of the *Steinlager 2* crew showed a marked contrast to that of the twenty-two young Kiwis who had arrived at Hamble four years earlier with *Lion New Zealand*. They were much quieter and a lot smarter, without the cockiness or over-confidence which the *Lion* crew had shown, although many of them were in that crew. This time, it seemed, they knew they had a special boat and were quietly confident that they could win, but they also knew that it was up to them to make sure that nothing went wrong. *Steinlager 2*'s work-up for the race was an object lesson to anyone who wishes to compete in a round-the-world race. The crew looked at the other boats at Hamble when they arrived and tried to assess their chances against each one of them; they had already built a database against *Fisher & Paykel* and knew how tough it was going to be to beat their fellow countrymen, all of whom were friends, some of them having sailed with Blake on *Lion New Zealand*. They sparred against *Satquote British Defender* and knew that they were better, but their joy was unbounded when they met *Rothmans* while running downwind with spinnakers set to

KZ
400
Fishe
SETTING

Grant Dalton, the tough young Kiwi skipper of *Fisher & Paykel*, who dogged Peter Blake every mile of the way to place second at his first attempt as skipper.

find that they were faster. Blake entered the 180-mile Channel Race to give the crew a taste of serious competition and, while no other Whitbread maxis were entered, there was the round-the-buoys maxi *Congère* to race against. *Steinlager 2* won the race both on line honours and on handicap. It may not have been much but it was a great morale booster. Then, when it came to the Fastnet, Blake insisted that *Steinlager 2* should use her old sails, keeping the new ones for the main event. When they were able to beat *Fisher & Paykel*, they knew they had a distinct advantage.

Grant Dalton was no less diligent in his preparation. The New Zealand white goods company, whose slogan 'The product is King', was almost certainly a driving force in the design and building of the 82ft ketch which was to bear the *Fisher & Paykel* name. Dalton was thorough in his preparation, launching the boat well in time, at the beginning of September 1988 after Marten Marine had completed her immaculate construction. Dalton, better than most, knew the value of sails and had secured the services of Tom Schnackenberg to design the driving force of his boat. 'Schnack' had the benefit of designing sails for the 90ft-waterline America's Cup challenger in which the technological limits had been severely stretched.

That there was always going to be a rivalry between *Fisher & Paykel* and *Steinlager 2* was understood from the moment that Dalton announced that he would enter this race. Dalton had been a watch-leader with Blake on *Lion New Zealand* and his friendship with the tall, blond New Zealander stretched back many years. Now they were face to face and, as the days to the start grew smaller, the friendly rivalry intensified.

Pierre Fehlmann, who had won the line-honours prize in the previous race with *UBS Switzerland*, carried race number one on *Merit*, another Farr-designed maxi, but alone among them, she was sloop rigged. The veteran of three previous Whitbreads believed in his own analysis of the conditions they were likely to face and felt the ketch rig was unsuitable.

For *Union Bank of Finland*, Ludde Ingvall, project manager of *Atlantic Privateer* in the previous race, had gone to Joubert and Nivelt for his design. Unlike many of the others, *UBF* had an aluminium hull although her deck was of high-tech composite construction. She was a big, powerful boat, perhaps of slightly heavy displacement, one of three yachts to come out of the small country of Finland. Markku Wiikeri went to Baltic Yachts for a maxi designed by German Frers, a boat which was subsequently to be shrouded by drama and with one of the strangest of keel configurations with the bulb protruding forwards from the fin. It was this keel which was to provide Wiikeri and his crew with severe problems. The third Finnish boat was Harry Harkimo's *Belmont Finland II*, the former *UBS Switzerland*. Harkimo, who had previously raced single-handed around the world, tackled the race on a relatively small budget.

Ireland is a small enough country to exude patriotic fervour and to be able to exploit that for fund raising for a Whitbread campaign. *NCB Ireland*, a Ron Holland design, was very definitely the heaviest displacement boat to come to the line. Skippered by Joe English, the green-and-white boat also had the longest boom of any of the competitors and this was to provide the Irish crew with their fair share of problems.

Most eyes that day were not on the maxis however; they were on the grey-hulled *Maiden*, the first boat ever in this race to be manned by an all-woman crew. The boat was not new. Built nine years earlier as *Disque d'Or III* for Pierre Fehlmann, the fifty-eight-footer, designed by Farr, was constructed in aluminium. Her skipper Tracy Edwards, who had sailed as cook on *Atlantic Privateer* and *Norsk Data GB* in the previous race, had spent months pestering potential sponsors and upholding her faith that women alone could handle this race. Her persistence, allied by her charm, told in the long run. She received sponsorship from the Royal Jordanian Airline and, unlike her American rival Nance Frank, was able to raise enough money to be on the line and know that *Maiden* had the funds to complete the race. The Duchess of York had expressed considerable interest in the *Maiden* project and was on board the start vessel.

Tracy was not alone in having a second-hand boat. Giorgio Falck purchased *NZI Enterprise* and refurbished it as *Gatorade*. He had two previous Whitbreads to his credit but never in a boat the size of this maxi-rater. Bruno Dubois was taking *Rucanor Sport* around for the second time as was Dirk Nauta with *Equity and Law*, formerly *Philips Innovator*. The winner, on handicap of the 1985/86 race was back again, racing for the third time as *L'Esprit de Liberté* with skipper Patrick Tabarly, while the all-time record went to *With Integrity*, the former *Great Britain II*, a boat which has never missed a Whitbread race.

Creighton's Naturally, her rival in the cruiser division, had sailed before as *FCF Challenger*; *Liverpool Enterprise*, Bob Salmon's charge this time, was previously *Atlantic Privateer*. *Schlussel von Bremen*, sponsored by Beck's, was a six-year-old Italian IOR racer, formerly known as *Sisisi*.

Daniel Mallé had approached his employers, the French post office, to sponsor the smallest entry in the race. The Bénéteau

The hull of *Fazisi* emerges from the fuselage of the Antonov AN124, the largest aircraft in the world, at Heathrow airport. Hastily built and underfunded she was held together by the strength of Skip Novak's resolve.

51, a Frers design named *La Poste*, was bound to bring up the rear, but it had the support of all the post office employees and was crewed entirely from that workforce. Mallé was able to joke as the race progressed that he and his crew had more fun than any other competitor because they took longer about it.

There had always been a threat that an ultra-light displacement boat would do well, at least on the Southern Ocean legs, and both the Spanish *Fortuna Extra Lights* and the French *Charles Jourdan* were to exploit this avenue. *Fortuna* was designed by Javier Visiers and displaced a mere twenty-three tons; she was skippered by Jan Santana and included Olympic medallist Jose Luis Doreste in her crew. *Charles Jourdan* rated seventy feet but was only seventy-two feet long compared with *Steinlager 2*'s eighty-six feet. The design by Guy Ribadeau-Dumas scaled in at under sixteen tons, half the displacement of *Steinlager 2*. She was skippered by Alain Gabbay who was unlucky not to win the third Whitbread race.

Mastercard, Eurocard and Access jointly sponsored the Swedish maxi ketch, *The Card*, skippered by Roger Nilson. The Bruce Farr maxi was the smallest of the ketches and masthead-rigged. She had initially been designed and built, by Eric Goetz, for Skip Novak, but when his sponsors failed to produce the necessary money, his former navigator Nilson took over the project. Nilson had with him as co-skipper Magnus Olsson, the two of them having been members of the *Drum* crew in the previous race. *The Card* lacked for nothing except perhaps the extra waterline length and sail area of the other two Farr ketches. Russia came into the Whitbread for the first time and to Glasnost and Perestroika, the word Fazisi was the next to be associated with Soviet Russia's international accord. It was the name of the Russian yacht and taken from an old name of a river in Georgia into which Jason sent the Argonauts in search of the Golden Fleece and in much the same way as that mythological hero, Valdislav Murnikov and his crew planned to find their equivalent of untold riches.

The Fazis Company, which put the first money into the project, is a joint-venture trading company owned by Russian and German interests. Its roubles enabled Murnikov to build the hull of the boat in aluminium. That hull was loaded aboard an Antonov AN124, the world's largest airplane, and flown to Heathrow before being taken to Hamble for fitting out. Murnikov had one lucky break for his project. He was visited by Dennis Conner when the America's Cup skipper was touring the USSR following the announcement that there was to be a Russian challenger for the Cup. Conner introduced the project to the attention of Pepsi-Cola and the company agreed to sponsor the boat until the start of the race.

Skip Novak was approached to coach the Russian crew and they realised that he was too good a proposition to let slip through their fingers and appointed him co-skipper.

***Rothmans'* skipper Lawrie Smith and his wife-to-be, Penny. Opposite: the low freeboard of Russia's *Fazisi* allows plenty of water to come aboard.**

Communication was something of a problem for Novak – his Russian vocabulary at the start stood at twelve words. *Fazisi* ran the gauntlet of a welter of problems, principally those of measurement and safety immediately prior to the race. A keel swap was organised, *Rothmans* donating their old one to the Russians, and Tony Castro from his nearby office providing the technical expertise to bring the Russian boat's rating down to seventy feet.

Money was the least of Lawrie Smith's worries and in that respect he was the envy of all the other twenty-three skippers. His virtually open-ended budget from the tobacco company Rothmans, was said to exceed $6 million. Rothmans had decided that, in its centenary year, a full-out attempt to win the race was appropriate and reversed the normal sequence of events, seeking designer and builder first, and finally the skipper. Smith was a natural choice as he was undoubtedly the most talented sailor in Britain with a great ability to pick and manage a team. He had placed fourth in the Soling class in the Olympics at Pusan and immediately gave his entire time to this project. Rothmans released him to be starting helmsman and tactician aboard the top-scoring *Jamarella*, in the Admiral's Cup. He said that the change was just what he needed, to re-stimulate his aggression, dulled by a break from competitive sailing.

Rothmans was designed by Rob Humphreys and without any initial input from Smith, he chose to go the sloop route. By the time Smith had joined the project, the boat was already too far down the road for any major changes to be made. Even so, no one at that time knew that the twin-masted configuration was a definite advantage. Smith and his crew spent many hours optimising the boat and going through a huge sail programme. There was, perhaps, no better-prepared boat than *Rothmans* even if she lacked some possible potential; certainly, no boat was better prepared to meet the media hype of the Whitbread race.

Prior to the start Peter Blake gave his crew their final briefing aboard the big red ketch and the message was painfully clear. They had a fast boat and it was up to them to make sure they got the result of which the boat was worthy.

The first leg was going to be the most important and a good result to Punta del Este could set any crew up for the whole race, but a bad one would have them on their back foot for the rest of the race, trying to make up time. Mike Quilter therefore had applied over three-quarters of his pre-race research to this leg of the race.

Everyone knew that the leg to Uruguay would be difficult because it would take a course through several major weather systems out to the trade winds and into the Doldrums, back into the trades and then an area of variables before reaching Punta. Few, however, would have expected boats to run into problems before the reached The Needles, but *Satquote British Defender*, and *NCB Ireland* both brushed the Shingles bank while *Schlussel von Bremen* lodged there for a full ten minutes.

Soon the Solent and the English Channel were behind them and most thoughts of England dimmed until the finish eight months away. By the time the light was waning, *Steinlager 2* was already a mile ahead of *Fisher & Paykel* and the fleet trailed behind the two New Zealand ketches. By the next morning the leaders were off Ushant and, in the daylight, the Kiwi crews could ascertain that three of the sloops, *Rothmans*, *Merit* and *UBF*, had overtaken them by the simple expedient of dodging a foul tide close along the French shore.

All the leaders went through the inshore passage, aided by a favourable six-knot current. It was to be a long day for the crew of *Steinlager 2*, aiming to reel the sloops in, but it was relatively easily achievable. The ketches were reaching three-quarters of a knot faster than the sloops. If it hadn't been evident before, it was now, that the sloops' crews were going to have to work very hard to stay in contention with the ketches. By nightfall, *Steinlager 2* was sixteen miles ahead of *Fisher & Paykel* and the fleet again trailed behind them.

In the morning, however, the Kiwi crew were given a big shock. They were blasting out to sea under an eighty-five per cent spinnaker, reefed main and mizzen staysail when they spotted a sail on the western horizon on a converging course. It turned out to be Rothmans with a poled-out No. 2 genoa. The two boats converged, each surfing at 20 knots and *Rothmans* passed two boat-lengths astern of *Steinlager 2* and continued to sail towards the Portuguese coast.

That crossing, with the Kiwis determinedly holding their starboard tack out to the west, may well have been the telling moment of the race. Going further west than the rest of the fleet gave *Steinlager 2* a huge advantage which she was not to lose. Peter Blake and Mike Quilter, deep in the bowels of the red ketch, poured over the weather maps delivered in a constant stream from the fax machine and were running them through the Apple MacWinds routeing programme. Their own desire to go west was confirmed by the computer.

It needed conviction to stick with it. *Steinlager 2* was the farthest out to the west but by the sixth day she was thirty miles ahead of *Merit*, the only other boat to have gone anywhere near

HH

KZ-2
Steinlager

as far to the west, and much further ahead of *Fisher & Paykel* and *Rothmans*. Still the wind blew for Blake while the boats further inshore had less. After a week at sea, with a spinnaker constantly set, *Steinlager 2* was 1,900 miles down the track and entering the tropics, well to the southwest of the Canary Islands.

After ten days of racing, *Steinlager 2* was 270 miles ahead of the next boat, *Fisher & Paykel* – under most circumstances, that would be more than a day in hand. But then the breeze went into the south and fell away to nothing. 'Big Red' was parked in what her crew believed to be the beginning of the Doldrums, but it was a 'private patch' caused by a hurricane building to the west. Little more than a day later and *Merit* was within fifty miles of the leader.

As luck would have it, the lead was to be restored to *Steinlager 2* as she picked her way through the Doldrums with greater alacrity than her rivals. After a fortnight the four leading maxis, *Steinlager 2*, *Merit*, *Fisher & Paykel* and *Rothmans*, were beginning to stretch their lead over the others. Way behind them, Tracy Edwards noted in *Maiden*'s log: 'Things are looking good. *Steinlager 2* is out of the Doldrums; they could be in Punta in twelve days.'

Steinlager 2 held herself out to the west and passed close by the Brazilian penal island of Fernando de Noronha, the first sight of land her crew had seen for fourteen days since Cape Finisterre and they were pleased with the progress they were making through the Trade Winds. Thirty knots of breeze has its own way of making sailing exciting.

At the start of the fourth week, the leader was to the east of Rio de Janeiro with around 1,000 miles to go to Punta. The wind was northerly and blowing at thirty-five knots; the conditions were ideal for fast passage-making and the Kiwi crew were riding on a high. 'Sailing through the night surfing down waves at twenty-two knots, the sensation is not a lot different to the Space Mountain rollercoaster ride at Disneyland,' wrote Glen Sowry of the experience. But it wasn't to last for ever and while the crew had been calculating their ETA in Punta, the numbers changed abruptly when a depression came through.

Then it was headwinds for 600 miles and, in the fresh wind, *Steinlager 2* carried only a No. 5 jib and a triple-reefed mainsail. The temperature dropped with the wind coming all the way from the Antarctic ice cap. At times the seas were so bad that Blake decided to ease the motion by taking the headsail down and nursed the ketch along, safe in the knowledge that he had a comfortable buffer over the rest.

For those without the buffer, there were some desperate moments. *Fisher & Paykel* had lost her mizzen a week before when she was in the strong northerlies with 1,000 miles to go, and *Rothmans*, which Lawrie Smith was pressing unmercifully, fell off the back of one wave with a startling crunch and cracked the deck alongside the runner winch. After that, even Smith had to ease up. *Steinlager 2* crossed the line in Punta early in the morning and was eleven-and-a-half hours ahead of *Merit* and almost thirty-two hours in front of *Fisher & Paykel*, the rival her crew most feared. *Rothmans* was another three-and-a-half hours further back. Lessons had been learned on the British sloop – the attempt to sail with a smaller crew than the others

Skip Novak, the American co-skipper of *Fazisi*, opens the champagne at Punta del Este at the end of the first leg from Southampton. Opposite: 'Big Red' – *Steinlager 2*.

had not been successful.

It was another day before *The Card* was fifth to finish but seven hours after her came the photo-finish between *Fazisi* and *Gatorade*. The Russian boat was just two minutes and forty seconds ahead of the Italians after 5,938 miles and only thirty-four minutes in front of *Martela* and an hour ahead of *Satquote British Defender*.

Equity and Law, the sole class C boat, was fifteenth to finish, ahead of *Liverpool Enterprise* and the cruising division maxis, *Creighton's Naturally* and *With Integrity*. *L'Esprit de Liberté* and *Rucanor Sport* beat *Maiden* in, the French boat taking the handicap prize. *La Poste*, the last to finish, took twelve days more than *Steinlager 2*.

The first stop-over will always be remembered for its tragedies. Alexei Grischenko, the co-skipper of *Fazisi*, with Skip Novak, had been under pressure for a long while. It boiled to a head not long after *Fazisi* finished and he disappeared. After twenty-four hours, Novak instigated a search for him with the help of Rear Admiral Charles Williams. A day-and-a-half later, Novak was called into Williams' office and informed, 'Your chap's been found – hanged himself in the woods.'

Novak was devastated by the reality of something he had half expected. Nevertheless he had to keep the project together and that required a mixture of diplomacy and strength with a crew, with many of whom he could ill communicate – a formidable task. It says much for Novak that *Fazisi* started the second leg.

Janne Gustavsson, one of the popular figures of the Whitbread, was involved in a motor-cycle accident. He was taken to hospital in a coma, declared 'brain dead' and the life support system switched off at the request of his family. *The Card* crewman's death cast an even greater pall over the fleet, most knew him well and missed this extrovert Swede immensely.

Sorting and packing headsails on *Satquote British Defender*, the Joint Services entry. Opposite: tucking the reef in neatly on *Rothmans*, the 80ft maxi skippered to fourth place by Lawrie Smith.

When the yachts began to arrive in Punta, the place was virtually closed. The town is a holiday resort, mainly for Argentines, and the season had yet to begin. Only the persistence of the crews and the Whitbread Race organisers succeeded in waking the sleepy town. By the time the fleet re-started, Punta was in full swing.

The awakening of the Uruguayan resort was not the only change experienced. Lawrie Smith had decided that there was a need for three more people aboard *Rothmans*. David Powys was already scheduled to join for the Southern Ocean legs but Smith wanted to reinforce the boat's crew with other top-calibre men. The bars of Punta were where he looked and it wasn't too difficult to recruit for *Rothmans* – there was a big budget and the possibility of doing well. Gordon Maguire and Henri Hiddes were not exactly enchanted with the way things had been going on *NCB Ireland* and decided to make the change. Some harsh words were said at the time but Smith got the men he wanted; Maguire, who had sailed with him on *Jamarella* in the Admiral's Cup, came as a helmsman, and Hiddes, a South African Whitbread veteran, to strengthen the crew.

Four days before the restart, a crewman with three previous Whitbreads under his belt and a large quantity of lubricating fluid inside him, spoke his mind. 'I've already been down to the Southern Ocean six times. I should have learned my lesson, but for some reason I keep going back.' He went on to detail the privations which turn human beings into little more than animals; conditions which stretch physical ability and relationships to breaking point. He took a long swig from the rum-and-coke that was never out of his hand. 'What does it matter if I get drunk tonight? From midday on Saturday I'll be drying out for a month.'

Alcohol and the Southern Ocean are immiscible. Down there, in the Roaring Forties, every faculty suffers in the penetrating cold, and further reduction by alcohol would be positively dangerous. *Rothmans*' meteorologist, David Houghton, suggested that 55 degrees south would be the best latitude, where the optimum track would be, but that the winds there might be too strong. The untrammelled winds can exceed 100 knots and this is beyond the limit for racing yachts. Yet for every degree further south they go, there is a saving of close to 200 miles – almost a day's run to the leading boats.

Day after day of zero temperatures and the biting chill factor of the gale-force winds are compensated by sailing that can be found nowhere else. It is the world of the slithering sleigh-ride down the faces of ten-storey waves that crest a third of a mile apart and which can drive the maxis at more than thirty knots – waves that can toss a thirty-five-ton yacht on its beam ends in a second. It is those waves which are the narcotic to the men and women, like the rum-and-coke drinker, in the Whitbread.

There was nothing that floated left in Punta harbour on the day of the re-start. The whole of the Uruguayan Navy was there.

Creighton's Naturally, formerly _FCF Challenger_, added extra ballast to qualify for the cruiser division. Tragedy was to strike in the Southern Ocean: man overboard.

The frigate *General Artegas* was at one end of the start-line and the two patrol boats that complete the fighting force afloat were there to clear a path. The three-masted schooner *Capitan Miranda* was the official starting boat and aboard her was the Duchess of York.

There was a six-mile leg to a turning mark, which should have been to windward but the wind conspired to make it a close reach with sheets cracked. Dalton appeared to have won the start at the weather end, leading Joe English and *NCB Ireland* away. Bunched with them were *Fortuna Extra Lights*, *Martela*, *Merit* and *Belmont Finland* with *The Card*, *Rothmans*, *Fazisi*, *Charles Jourdan* and *Equity & Law*. Peter Blake wanted to keep clear of the ruck and started in mid-line, reaching down to gain speed and hardening up at twelve knots on the gun. There were two of those – a recall – and no one returned. A full eight minutes passed before *Fisher & Paykel*, sailing neck-and-neck with *Steinlager 2*, hardened up, tacked and went back to the line. Her impetuosity had cost her a valuable quarter of an hour.

The start may have been a relatively gentle affair on 28 October, but that night the crews received a foretaste of what they might expect. The wind came aft and blew strongly. The leaders blasted down the waves, surfing at over twenty knots. Three days later, *Steinlager 2* was hard on the wind while *Fisher & Paykel*, *Rothmans* and *Merit* which had gone further south, were reaching as a result of a low-pressure system. Those three, *F&P* in particular, gained a jump on the fleet. Blake reported: 'Conditions are becoming very gruelling,' with force eight to nine winds, highly confused seas and snow showers.

Fisher & Paykel led *Rothmans* by fifty-four miles and *Fortuna Extra Lights* was four miles astern of the British sloop after nine days. *Rothmans* had been forced to replace her plastic headfoil when the first one shattered in the cold, close to 50 degrees south. Two weeks into the race and an accident aboard *Fisher & Paykel* underlined the dangers. The spinnaker halyard block at the base of the mast exploded and the snatch load jerked the halyard winch off the deck. It flew head-high across the deck at the mast. Fortunately, there was no one in the way.

Rothmans had twice broken her spinnaker pole, while there was even greater damage on *NCB Ireland*. Her main boom had broken and progress was slower while the crew worked feverishly with limited tools and equipment to repair it. Tracy Edwards and her all-woman crew in *Maiden* were leading the small boat class by eighty-four miles.

Disaster was to hit *Creighton's Naturally* at 0322 on Sunday 12 November. In big seas, towering some sixty feet above the deck, the eighty-foot boat gybed involuntarily. The running backstay broke and the yacht gybed again. The mainsheet looped around two of the grinder pedestals and ripped them off the deck. The mainsail was taken down and another backstay was being set up when the yacht was hit by two very large waves and the headsail, which was boomed out, was set aback as the boat broached on the second wave, breaking the spinnaker boom.

Anthony Phillips and Bart van den Dwey were swept overboard, each wearing a lifejacket equipped with flares and personal radio beacons. Two life belts and a dan-buoy were dropped and the VHF direction-finder for their personal beacons operated. All sails were lowered and the boat motored back to where the men had gone overboard. Van den Dwey was sighted with the aid of a white parachute flare and recovered after forty-seven minutes in the water. He was successfully resuscitated. Phillips was next aboard and resuscitation attempted unsuccessfully for three hours.

It is believed that Phillips hit one of the guardrail stanchions as he went overboard and may have been unconscious as he hit the water, which would account for his lifejacket not being inflated.

Two crew members, Barry Mercer and Julian Morris, went into the sea three times to assist with the recovery of the men. Skipper John Chittenden described their actions as 'heroic'. Van den Dwey suffered shock and mild hypothermia but was soon on the way to recovery. Phillips was buried at sea in the ocean that had claimed his life.

Chittenden sent this tragic account of the death of his watch-leader from the yacht:

'At 0322 on Sunday the yacht gybed heavily running before a westerly gale. The weather runner broke and the yacht gybed again, breaking two winch grinder pedestals.

The mainsail was taken down and the lee runner was rapidly being set up when we were hit by two very huge seas at 0345. The yacht broached on the second sea and the poled-out yankee was set aback, breaking the spinnaker pole.

Two men, Bart van den Dwey and Tony Phillips, were swept overboard. Both men were equipped with lifejackets, flares and personal EPIRBs. Two liferings and the dan-buoys were thrown overboard and the direction-finder (used to track the signals from the personal EPIRBs) operated. The headsails were dropped and the yacht motored back on the direction-finding bearing to the men. The first man was located with the aid of white parachute flares at 0415. The first man, Bart van den Dwey was recovered and successfully resuscitated at 0432. Tony Phillips was recovered and resuscitation started and continued until 0717 without success. Bart's lifejacket was inflated but Tony Phillips' was not.

Tony Phillips hit a stanchion as he went overboard and it is thought unlikely that he was conscious once in the water. The two EPIRBs were recovered but the two life-rings and dan-buoys were not.

Two crew-members, Barry Mercer and Julian Morris went into the sea three times to assist with their recovery. Both actions were, in my opinion, heroic – Julian's in particular.'

Six days later, Markku Wiikeri was benefiting from his heavy gamble in going further south than the rest. The Finn appeared to be on a winning streak with *Martela* but the meteorological chips were stacked against him. *Martela* was 225 miles south of *Fisher & Paykel*; Dalton had had to go north to the Kerguelen Islands and that lost him quite a bit of his once-huge lead when he

CREIGHTONS®
Naturally

MAIDEN

lost most of the wind for a day. The leading eight boats had closed to where just sixty miles covered them in terms of distance left to the finish and all of them knew that the lighter winds were only temporary; more was forecast and plenty of it.

The depression which brought the stronger westerlies with it moved north and the Finns found themselves beating to windward, while *F&P* and *Fortuna* scampered on. In twenty-four hours, *Fortuna* gained forty miles on *Fisher & Paykel* and drew up to within four miles astern. A final blast sent *Fortuna* scuttling into a short-lived lead. With a record run of 398 miles from noon to noon followed by a twenty-four-hour run from 1100 the following day of 405 miles she became the first monohull to break the magic 400-mile day. Dalton had, by then, tracked the Spaniard on the radar and watched as *Fortuna* drew ahead with 1,855 miles to go to Fremantle. It all ended in tears when Rafael Tibua broke his leg against the mast after being washed down the foredeck by breaking water. Two bones close to the ankle were broken. The leg was set in a Kevlar plaster, but on arrival in Australia he was flown home for surgery to correct the set of the bones. A few miles behind them was the chasing pack of *Charles Jourdan*, *Steinlager 2*, *Rothmans* and *Merit*. *Martela*, in two days, had dropped back to tenth place.

On 22 November, the four leaders, *Fisher & Paykel*, *Rothmans*, *Merit* and *Steinlager 2*, were in line abreast, heading north-east. All four skippers were agreed that the outcome would be decided on the movement of the high-pressure area. 'It's a matter of who has the right line past the high,' said Dalton, with Blake adding: 'Finding a way through the lighter winds will decide who wins the leg.'

With just over 300 miles to go, *Rothmans* took the lead but *Merit* was right with her, just a mile behind. They were closest to the coast, hoping for the sea-breeze, for which this coastline is justly famous. The final stages of the second leg were fought out in darkness and mystery as the four yachts closed on the Fairway buoy in Gage Roads, to the north-east of Rottnest Island, just twelve miles from the finishing line. Early the previous morning, *Steinlager 2* took over the lead when it most counted and kept her position secret as darkness fell. *Fisher & Paykel* had 'parked' and *Steinlager 2*, in three hours, had gone from behind to in front with a gain of twenty-six miles.

It was still dark when *Steinlager 2* crossed the line, the huge cannon booming out from the end of the harbour wall. As dawn broke, the next two boats appeared with hardly a gap between them as they rounded the fairway buoy. *Merit* was ahead of *Rothmans* and a match-race was on to the finish. Smith urged all he could out of crew and boat and beat *Merit* to the line by twenty-eight seconds, a narrow enough margin after 7,650 miles of racing and just an hour-and-a-half down on the winner. Another hour-and-a-half passed before *Fisher & Paykel*, the leader for most of the leg, came in to finish fourth.

Charles Jourdan and *The Card* were next, fourteen hours later and the floodgates were open for a constant stream of finishers. It was eight days after *Steinlager 2* that *Maiden* finished, ahead of all her class. Tracy Edwards and her crew had produced a performance which stripped away the last vestiges of patronage from everyone. Bob Fisher, who had described the aluminium boat with its all-woman crew as a 'Tinful of tarts' had modified it to a 'Tinful of smart tarts,' after the first leg, changed it, with some grace, to a 'Tinful of fast, smart tarts'.

***Maiden*'s ladies show their form as they sail into Fort Lauderdale, at the end of the fifth leg. The pose guaranteed them publicity but infuriated feminists.**

What the *Maiden* crew had achieved, was quite remarkable. They were thirty hours ahead of *Rucanor Sport*, *Schlussel von Bremen* and *L'Esprit de Liberté*, all of whom finished in a twelve-minute period. *Maiden* had won the leg on corrected time by sixteen hours and it put her in the overall lead in class D after the first two legs. As part of the recognition for that performance, Tracy was awarded the Dennis P Miller Trophy by the Royal Ocean Racing Club for the best performance in the year by any British yacht racing abroad.

Each crew had their own tales of woe, the most remarkable being the rescue of Rasmas Schmidt from *Schussel von Bremen*, who was flicked overboard by a whipping spinnaker sheet three weeks before.

The accident occurred as they were changing spinnakers in the dead of night. 'The sail suddenly filled, I hadn't got my harness clipped on and I was pushed overboard' he recalled. Despite the shock and intense cold of the freezing waters, Schmidt had the presence of mind to hold a pocket torch to his head to guide the crew back.

'I did panic a little, but tried to tell myself to remain calm. The crew were very quick. The helmsman shouted "man overboard" and turned the boat round immediately, while the others rushed to take down the spinnaker. I never lost sight of them, or they of me, and I was picked up within three minutes. I was very lucky to have been sailing with such a good crew.'

On board *Rucanor* four crew were injured at one time when the yacht's boom broke. 'One cut his fingers, two others hurt an arm and leg and one landed on his coccyx when the boat lurched violently,' skipper Bruno Dubois explained. The injuries left *Rucanor*'s six remaining crew with the task of making repairs and sailing the boat. 'We fell more than 150 miles behind *Maiden* in two days and morale sank to an all-time low,' said Dubois.

Patrick Tabarly, skipper of *L'Esprit de Liberté*, who lost contact with his sponsor and race funds during the first stage of the race to Uruguay, blamed their performance on poor preparation. 'We only knew five days before the re-start that we could continue the race,' he said.

They blew out five spinnaker poles during the voyage, but on accumulative time remained second, sixteen hours and twenty-four minutes behind *Maiden* with *Rucanor* a further hour astern. 'The girls sailed a very good race' Tabarly conceded.

Andrew Coghill and his crew on *With Integrity* finished bowed, but far from broken, after a traumatic thirty-seven-day voyage across the Southern Ocean in their veteran British maxi. Skipper Coghill refuted the claims of two former crew-mates who said that the yacht was not seaworthy after being left ashore at the start of this leg from Punta.

'Yes, the radio did not work, and she is not in the best condition, but I'm the best judge of whether the yacht is seaworthy or not, and I'm not about to risk my neck. The boat will get all the

The first boat in the race to exceed 400 miles in 24 hours, the Javier Viziers-designed *Fortuna Extra Lights*.

***UBF* leads *NCB* as the fleet sails away from Fremantle, back into the Southern Ocean via Cape Horn. Opposite: foredeck work aboard the Farr-designed ketch, *The Card*.**

way round,' Coghill, a former lifeboat coxwain from Aberdovey, Wales asserted.

Despite the breakages, the most traumatic moment for the crew came on 14 November when Willie Bridel, the yacht's engineer fell overboard. 'It happened in daylight during a change of watch when we were setting a spinnaker. He came on deck and was standing on the spinnaker sheet when the sail suddenly filled and flicked him overboard.'

'He took his boots off and after scooping air into them, held them under his arms to keep himself afloat. The crew cut the spinnaker and sheets away, and we sailed back to pick him up.'

The crew had just spotted their first iceberg, and with the water near freezing their engineer was close to unconsciousness when they recovered him twenty-five minutes later. 'It was a close thing, and some of the girls were in tears about it, but we carried him below and warmed him up and now he is perfectly alright,' Coghill confirmed.

Kim Slater, the sailmaker, whose voyage was sponsored by British Telecom, said, 'it has been a tremendous experience, but there were many times when I was very worried, and frightened.' With no sewing machine onboard, however, Slater had plenty to keep her mind occupied, repairing the many damaged sails by hand.

Their biggest problems, however, came when a steering wire broke and jammed in its sheeve. The boat broached, and the boom snapped in two when it crashed against the shroud. To make the repair, the crew cut two feet off one of the spinnaker poles to form an internal sleeve and fastened the spar together with bolts removed from fittings on the deck.

Fremantle was a time of wound-licking after the rigours of the Southern Ocean. Boats were put right and crews relaxed in the town where two years earlier the America's Cup had taken place. It was a time and place to warm up in preparation for the 'sprint' to Auckland, the halfway point of the race, where the sailors traditionally receive a phenomenal welcome.

Someone had to be a sadist to decide that the re-start from Fremantle should be two days before Christmas; it would mean that both that day and New Year's Eve would be spent at sea. Many had felt that a Boxing Day start would have been better but no one was listening at race headquarters.

The day was a rainy one with a westerly breeze, a direction at least that was to please the crews as it meant that they fast reached away towards Cape Leeuwin rather than be hard on the wind. As an hors d'oeuvre, there was a short leg from the start in towards Cottesloe beach, where many of the crews had relaxed in the company of the local girls, before a short beat to round the northern end of Rottnest Island. Pierre Fehlmann took *Merit* out of the start-line to lead *Steinlager 2* and *Fisher & Paykel* around the first mark with *Rothmans* in close attendance. Across Gage Roads the order remained the same and then as the fleet began to head southwards, the wind increased to thirty-five knots.

The race was on again. The boats were blasting their way south around Cape Leeuwin and into the Great Australian Bight on the 3,434-mile leg. Speeds were high and the competition intense. *Merit* held the lead for more than a day, but when the reaching began in earnest, the ketches went to the front. Not for long. Once again the light-displacement boats came into their own with Alain Gabbay in *Charles Jourdan* surfing through to the front. At noon on Boxing Day, the French sloop was nine miles ahead of the Kiwi ketches. The day before, *Fortuna* had pulled up to be level with *Steinlager 2* and then wiped out in spectacular fashion.

Charles Jourdan's lead was slowly whittled away and the following day saw *Fisher & Paykel*, the front-runner, dicing closely with *Steinlager 2*. *F&P* continued to lead around Tasmania and into the Tasman Sea. New Year's Eve was a bad dream for the leaders, 'parked' close to the inappropriately (then) named Storm Bay. *Merit* closed sixty miles that day and the front running became more tense. As 1990 dawned, *Rothmans* also began to close and two days later with 245 miles to go to the Auckland finish, nine miles covered the first three boats. *Steinlager 2* led *Fisher & Paykel* by four miles with *Rothmans* in third place; *Merit* was just eleven miles further back and the group was headed for Cape Reinga at the tip of the North Island of New Zealand.

In the meantime, there had been a radio call from Alain Gabbay to the race headquarters telling of *Charles Jourdan*'s encounter with a sperm whale. The collision resulted in a ten-foot-long hole in the starboard side of the boat which the French crew had to patch as best they could. Had the hole, caused by the impact of the tail fin of the whale, been any closer to the waterline,

Charles Jourdan would undoubtedly have sunk.

At Cape Reinga, *Steinlager 2* led by three miles and Blake cancelled the watch system. He knew that to keep a fired-up *Fisher & Paykel* crew behind would need full-time effort on the part of all fifteen men on board the big red ketch. No New Zealand boat had ever led the race into Auckland and both skippers and their crews were determined to claim that honour. Once round the North Cape, as night began to fall, the wind began to freshen. The navigation lights went out on *F&P* and only came on again when a radio call from *Steinlager 2* reminded her crew that they were obliged to show them. Dalton had tried to give Blake the slip. In the morning *Fisher & Paykel* was still astern but brought up a further freshening breeze to be within a hundred metres of the leader as the boats had forty miles to go.

Spectator boats had begun to gather and Blake, on the wheel, looked behind at a stormy sky over Auckland. He ordered Mike Quilter to search the radio for any indication as to what might happen. As Quilter switched on he heard a caller in Titirangi talk of a southerly front going through. Blake's answer was to call for a small genoa to be made ready and the crew to be prepared for a quick dousing of the spinnaker and mizzen staysail. The instant that the wind change was sighted, a mile ahead, Blake called for the sail change and the boys made it just before the forty-knot squall hit. Dalton and his crew were caught with their trousers down and their spinnaker up. Blake looked briefly over this shoulder and said with some satisfaction: 'Got the bastards.' Suddenly the gap between them was a mile and *Steinlager 2* was on her way to a phenomenal welcome in her home port.

Six minutes and four seconds separated the two Kiwi ketches and an hour later *Merit* led *Rothmans* in by ten minutes. Thirteen boats finished in twenty-four hours with the dismasted *UBF* limping in a day later under jury rig. Two and a half days

***Merit* and *Rothmans* alongside the Princes Wharf in Auckland after finishing ten minutes apart thanks to smart tactical work by *Rothmans'* skipper Lawrie Smith.**

after the first finisher, *Maiden* crossed the line, leader and handicap winner of class D, another sensational triumph for Tracy Edwards and her all-woman crew. Her reward came when a few days later she received the British Yachtsman of the Year Trophy. It was presented by Peter Blake. The six-foot-four-inch blond Kiwi sailor and his crew were to receive the New Zealand Yachtsman of the Year Trophy a few days later.

At Auckland in the long stop-over, some of the boats were hauled out, their rigs removed and checked and their rudders drawn for examination. It kept the crews out of too much mischief, although visits to Dick Jones' pub were relatively frequent, and away from the bungy-jumping – the craze sweeping New Zealand – but many of the sailors had a go anyway.

The fourth leg, 5,914 miles to Punta del Este, took the fleet once again down into what Lawrie Smith had dubbed 'The Sea of Certain Death' to the most feared landmark of yachtsmen, Cape Horn, situated at 57 degrees south. The prospect was in everyone's mind on 4 February, the day after the Commonwealth Games had finished, when the second half of the race began. Almost all of Auckland's population had turned out to watch the start off North Head.

In the lightish airs, it was difficult for any boat to make a good showing. *UBF*, with a new mast, *Merit* and *Rothmans* were all well placed in the short first leg before they headed out to sea. Seven minutes after the start *The Card* snagged her mizzen in the rigging of a forty-foot ketch moored to watch the spectacle. The smaller boat was hauled right over but *The Card*'s mizzen snapped. Skipper Roger Nilson made the decision to dump the mizzen rig into the sea (where it was later collected) and continue in the race. Originally he planned to meet up with the repaired rig at Chatham Island, but it was too badly damaged for a repair to be effected in time and for the rest of the leg the Swedish boat was a sloop.

Not that it appeared to be too much of a handicap; in the light airs off Cape Colville, *The Card* picked up a little extra breeze and sailed round the entire fleet and into the lead.

Unsurprisingly, the two Kiwi ketches soon pulled out into the lead as they made their way southeast to a latitude of 53 degrees south. Shorts and tee-shirts soon gave way to thermal gear and balaclavas as the temperature dropped sharply. The pace was up; daily runs of more than 300 miles were clocked regularly.

Four days into the race, Bruno Dubois' *Rucanor Sport* was in collision with a whale and there was damage to the rudder and the stern of the boat. *Rucanor Sport* was forced to return to New Zealand for repairs and, because of light airs later, when she had resumed the race, she had to motor to Punta del Este to be there in time for the re-start and thus retired from this leg.

Smith was gambling, as he had predicted, by going further south than the rest. He wanted fresh westerlies for just the running conditions in which *Rothmans* had proved faster than the ketches. 'We are now a day behind,' he said in Auckland, 'and that means we can no longer hope to beat *Steinlager 2* and *Fisher & Paykel* by boat speed, particularly when they are faster than us in most conditions. What we have to do is take a calculated flyer and go for what we believe are better winds in order that we can jump a complete weather pattern on them.'

He tried, but the Kiwis still held sway, particularly when the wind went into the north and was lighter. When there were westerlies, *Rothmans* did hold sway but *Charles Jourdan* was faster than them all. She had, by the time she found the right winds, more than enough to catch up but moved from seventh to fourth on the ninth day, behind the ketches and *Rothmans*. *Maiden*'s success was eluding her. The all-woman crew were seventy-six miles astern of *L'Esprit de Liberté* and a few days later were reduced in strength when Mikaela von Kuskull was injured when the boom hit her head, leaving her unconscious for five minutes. Six days later with Mikki back in business with a vengeance, Michele Parat was rather more badly injured when a

***The Card* snags her mizzen on a spectator boat at the re-start in Auckland. The incident confirmed the organisers' worst fears. No one was hurt and she managed to sail the leg, not unsuccessfully, as a sloop.**

huge wave swept over *Maiden*'s deck and bent her backwards against the wheel. The boat broached, water poured down below and the generator went out of action.

Michele had to be strapped into her bunk and Claire Russell, the doctor on board, had a serious patient on her hands. Roger Nilson, an orthopaedic surgeon, offered what help he could from *The Card* and other boats offered to turn round to help in any way. That led Claire and Tracy to a philosophical discussion as to why men would do that when they wouldn't even open a door for them ashore. Michele's recovery was slow; it was four days before she was back on deck, and then doing very little.

The race to the Horn was in full flight, spearheaded by *Steinlager 2*, which carried an 'extra crewman.' Frederick Chapman had rounded the Cape in 1924 aboard the barquentine *Garthneill* and had recently died in Auckland. His relatives asked Blake if he would convey his ashes to Cape Horn and scatter them.

Fisher & Paykel was only five miles astern of *Steinlager 2* when the leader rounded the southernmost point of South America. Blake read a short service and a prayer before committing 'Dusty' Chapman to the deep. It was the one break in concentration for the entire leg. *Steinlager 2* hustled on to the 'tidal gate' of the Strait de la Maire. It separates the Southern and Atlantic Oceans and always provides a bumpy ride; this time was no exception. There were still 1,400 miles to go to the finish and with each one of them the promise of warmer weather.

Once again the Kiwi ketches indulged in a match race and were almost at the finish when the radio receivers on both boats, and at race HQ, which had insisted on hourly radio reports, heard the emergency call emanate from *Martela*: 'Mayday, Mayday, the keel is falling off.' The keel of the Finnish boat had been the cause of concern on the fist leg and had been repaired when the boat was hauled out in Montevideo.

The radio operator's voice had a sense of panic about it. He gave the latitude of the yacht and then there was silence. The operator was at that moment rapidly climbing out the and up on to the upturned hull. The keel had indeed fallen off and the boat had capsized. *Merit* and *Charles Jourdan*, which were the two nearest boats, immediately went to the aid of *Martela*. They reached the stricken vessel and took the crew aboard their boats and set off again for Punta del Este 350 miles away.

At the time, *Steinlager 2* had only 150 miles to go to the finish. She arrived in Punta twenty-one minutes ahead of *Fisher & Paykel* and the two Kiwi crews set about celebrating together. *Rothmans* arrived early the next morning, twelve-and-a-half hours down on *Steinlager 2* and Smith led a very determined crew up the jetty, with little ceremony to the 'Rat Hole' – the sleaze bar closest to his boat. That morning's mini-drinkathon will go down in the annals of this race as being one to have stayed well clear of; strong men wilted.

It was some time later that *Merit* and *Charles Jourdan*

arrived, each credited with a time allowance for rescuing the crew of *Martela*. *UBF* was listed as sixth to finish, then came *Gatorade*, *The Card*, *NCB Ireland*, *Belmont Finland*, *Fortuna*, *British Defender* and *Fazisi*. *L'Esprit de Liberté* recovered the overall lead from *Maiden* in class D with *La Poste* finishing only three hours after the all-woman crew.

Having exhausted the opportunities of a Punta in full flood, the crews were well ready to go to sea again. Many more boats were out this time as the fleet started in light airs. Smith took *Rothmans* into the lead and adopted a very real approach to winning the leg. He had determined the strategy before leaving, with the help of meteorologist David Houghton, which was to go further east than the others would go and pick up favourable winds in the south east trades.

It was six days into the race before *Rothmans* had a twenty-mile lead over *Steinlager 2*, but then each day it stretched, until three days later the British boat was eighty miles in front and gaining, the 5,475-mile leg seemingly going Smith's way, at least in the early days. The Doldrums were still to come – the Equator was 500 miles away. But *Rothmans'* lead went almost as quickly as it had developed when a rather unusual weather system allowed the boats to the west of her to slip through around the northeast corner of the South American mainland. Once again, the two ketches were in command and as they approached Fort Lauderdale, after three weeks at sea, it was *Steinlager 2* that led *Fisher & Paykel*.

The 84ft red ketch stormed home in the early light of the morning, thirty-four-and-a-half minutes ahead of *Fisher & Paykel*. It was her fifth successive win. Fort Lauderdale was ready for Blake and his crew. The chef at the Pier 66 Hotel had heard that Blake fancied a hamburger and greeted him with one a full four feet six inches in diameter. Four hours after the Kiwis, *Rothmans* sailed in, more than thirteen hours ahead of *Merit* and thereby established the prospect of a battle royal for third place overall. The British boat had narrowed the Swiss boat's advantage while *Fisher & Paykel* took over second place.

It may not have been a good leg for *Maiden* – they finished fourth in class D – but the girls sure finished in style. They arrived in the early afternoon with all the crew on deck in swimsuits. That blew the minds of the American media. *Maiden* was also the scene of her project manager Howard Gibbons' wedding to Elizabeth Green, sister of Nancy Hill, one of the crew.

There were just 3,831 miles left to race to the finish at Southampton. For some, like *Steinlager 2*, thirty-five hours in the lead, it needed only to be a leg of consolidation. Dalton, when asked if he still thought he could win, answered, 'Has Peter Blake retired?' Others had scores to settle on the sprint home, notably *Rothmans* fighting for third place with *Merit*.

The start was marred by the presence of a US Coast Guard cutter, the size of a destroyer, which ploughed across the racers' path soon after the start. That aside, it was a perfect day of Florida sunshine and there were more than 4,000 craft, heavily marshalled by the Coast Guard, out to watch the twenty-two boats as they came to the line. Dirk Nauta in the 62ft *Equity & Law* made the best start while *Charles Jourdan* and *Rothmans* were recalled for being early. Once the maxis had passed the smaller boats, including *Maiden*, which had started better, it was *The Card* which set the pace closely followed by *Steinlager*.

The dramatic rescue of a crewman from the capsized Finnish maxi *Martela OF* by Pierre Fehlmann's *Merit*.

Blake had said that he was going to sail the last leg conservatively, but there was little sign of that in the early stages. He did avoid any chance of an incident when Nauta showed signs of luffing as *Steinlager 2* began to attack to windward; Blake just bore off and sailed through the smaller sloop to leeward. At the Hillsborough buoy, ten miles north of Fort Lauderdale, *Steinlager 2* was twenty-five seconds astern of *The Card* but as sure as day follows night, the Kiwi crew began to overhaul the Swedes and *Steinlager 2* was out in front.

Third around the mark was *Merit*, just a boat-length ahead of *Fisher & Paykel*. As the leaders rounded, the sky was thick with a dragonflies' tea party – the media helicopters and light aircraft were all homing in for the opportunity which the mark provided. Joe English in *NCB Ireland* and Ludde Ingvall in *UBF* were next before the fast-recovering *Rothmans*. *Fortuna Extra Lights* and *Belmont Finland* were close behind.

The race was not twelve hours old before there was a casualty. *Gatorade*'s skipper, Hervé Jan, radioed that the uppermost starboard spreader had collapsed and that they were heading for Jacksonville to effect a repair. The other boats were soon into the Gulf Stream and with it headwinds. The seas were nasty and the boats crashed to windward. On the second day out, disaster struck *Rothmans* when an intermediate rod shroud – the D3 – gave way. The crew were lucky to save the mast and they

Steinlager 2 with less than a mile to sail to the finish, surrounded by well wishers, powers up Southampton Water to the finish to post a clean sweep of results.

were forced to head for Georgetown to replace it. Two Lear Jets with a replacement rod and a repair crew flew to Georgetown to meet *Rothmans* and the turn-round time was just two hours – enough time for the crew to find the local McDonalds – but *Rothmans* was 280 miles astern of the leaders.

On the fourth day the wind moderated for the leaders and came astern, but progress was generally slow. *Fisher & Paykel* was to the north of *Steinlager 2* and generally seemed to be favoured. *Rothmans* had begun to roar across the ocean and was making up lost ground fast.

There was never much between the two leaders all the way across the Atlantic, Dalton choosing a more northerly route after the boats had left the warm Gulf Stream waters for the chilly Labrador Current. Blake had to keep a weather eye on *Merit*, to the south, as well and this ensured that *Steinlager 2* was always between them.

It was 0150 on the fifth day when a loud crack startled the entire *Steinlager 2* crew. The port mizzen chainplate had fractured. Brad Butterworth spun the wheel and crash-gybed the boat to put the load on the starboard shrouds in twenty knots of wind. The whole rig, not simply the mizzen, might have gone over the side as the main running backstays were anchored to the same chainplate. Feverishly the crew worked to have relief shrouds rigged and were bolting padeyes to the deck to act as makeshift chainplates. The red boat was slowed but so too were her rivals who suffered lighter winds during the night.

Two days later, *Satquote British Defender* was not so lucky. The topmast shroud failed and down came the top of her mast. Her race was virtually at an end, but skipper Colin Watkins organised a jury rig with all that he had available and sailed a less than fast passage back to Southampton, taking six-and-a-half days longer than the leader.

Fisher & Paykel had a ten-mile lead over *Steinlager 2*; *Merit* moved up to third, forty-five miles further back, while *NCB Ireland* slipped two places to fifth with *The Card* taking up fourth place. Fastest boat on the water was *Rothmans*, her crew trying desperately to catch up, helped by favourable breezes.

Fisher & Paykel's crew had their scary moment too. They came close to seeing their mizzen over the side for the second time when the mizzen forestay broke. There were icebergs about and the air and sea temperatures had dropped steeply.

It wasn't until the twelfth day out that the two leaders caught sight of each other. They had spent a very dark night in light winds and dawn found them about five miles apart with *Fisher & Paykel* the more northerly. The two boats split and it was *Fisher & Paykel* that was first to find the stronger breeze. The following day, *F&P* was three-and-a-half miles to leeward – *Steinlager* had made a significant gain. This match race was to continue all the way to the finish. At Lands End, *Steinlager 2* was three miles ahead but then became becalmed off the Lizard allowing *Fisher & Paykel* to sail up to within three boat-lengths. Then the breeze freshened and came from ahead; *Steinlager 2* moving back into a three-mile lead watched by the media in helicopters and light planes. Throughout the last night, the entire *Steinlager* crew were on deck, sitting on the rail, legs over the side in an effort to produce every last vestige of speed.

By the time the big red New Zealand ketch reached the Needles, *Fisher & Paykel* was far enough back that only a dismasting could rob Blake of his sixth successive Beefeater Trophy for winning the leg and with it the race. The spectator boats had begun to gather off Poole and, as *Steinlager 2* entered the western Solent, a small, rapidly growing armada was forming. Few bothered to drop back to see *Fisher & Paykel*; the boat that led the Whitbread fleet out of Hurst Narrows was leading them back in, the boat which had the happy knack of going to the front every time it really mattered. Southampton Water was packed almost solid with craft as the leader made her way to the finish. Then came that magic second when the cannon boomed out and Kiwi arms aboard 'Big Red' were raised in triumph. After seventeen years of trying, Peter Blake had finally won the Whitbread Trophy. The dockside scenes were joyous and noisy. As the *Steinlager 2* crew acknowledged the cheers, they turned round to cheer in 'their mates' on *Fisher & Paykel* who finished thirty-six minutes astern of them. The Kiwi rout was complete; two entries – first and second. Blake's phenomenal performance was to win him many accolades, including the award of the OBE in the New Year's Honours list, Tracy Edwards, for hers, was to receive the MBE.

In Ocean Village Marina, Blake stood on the deck with his wife, Pippa and his two children, Sarah and James, and said that it was his last Whitbread Race. 'I don't think my wife will have to lock me up when the next race comes around,' and, hugging his children, he added: 'I think these will keep me at home.' The last leg had been the toughest, according to him, 'not in the terms of the sailing but in terms of the nervous energy we had to spend. All the time we had a battle with *Fisher & Paykel* and they were never going to give up.' Dalton's first crack at the Whitbread as a skipper had brought him second place, one day, eleven hours and thirty-eight minutes down on his former skipper and friend. *Fisher & Paykel* had led for more than half of the last five days, but Blake and his crew always seemed to be able to summon up reserves of speed in the final stages.

It was early evening when Pierre Fehlmann brought *Merit* in two hours behind *Fisher & Paykel* and then there was a gap of ten hours to the early morning when *Rothmans* finally crossed the line, having been forced to kedge off Lymington when the wind died away completely and the ebb tide threatened to send them back out to the Needles. *Rothmans* was still six hours ahead of *The Card*, a remarkable performance after having to return to Georgetown. *Belmont Finland* and *Fortuna Extra Lights* were next with *Fazisi* eighth home ahead of *UBF*. *Equity and Law* produced a stunning finish ahead of *NCB Ireland*, *Gatorade*, *Charles Jourdan* and *Liverpool Enterprise*. *Creighton's Naturally* was next to win the cruiser class, while *Schlussel von Bremen* beat *L'Esprit de Liberté* home by twenty-four minutes but that did not stop the French boat from winning the class for this leg and overall. Just for once, *La Poste* was not last home, she beat the crippled *Satquote British Defender* and *With Integrity*. That much pleased Daniel Mallé and his crew.

Profile

Peter Blake

The jinx that has cost Peter Blake so much throughout his high-profile yachting career, was finally laid to rest during the 1989/90 Whitbread. The skipper of the New Zealand maxi *Steinlager 2* won the race at the fifth attempt in the most convincing manner, though victory came within a whisker of turning into yet another disaster.

A shroud plate holding both the mainmast and mizzen-masts pulled out of the boat four days after leaving Fort Lauderdale on the last leg, and it was only the quick thinking of helmsman Brad Butterworth in crash-gybing the yacht, that saved both masts from crashing down and ending Blake's career as it had begun – fighting adversity, failure and ill-fortune.

There have been successes, of course. The forty-two-year-old Aucklander is only the fourth man in history to win the line and handicap double in the Sydney to Hobart race, a 630-mile Australian ocean marathon of equal standing to Britain's equally notorious Fastnet, which he has also won twice.

In 1988 Peter Blake and his long-term crew-mate Mike Quilter, set a record for the 7,500-mile race round Australia when the main opposition was actually the weather, rather than the motley bunch of craft that followed in the wake of his multihull *Steinlager I*.

'Those were among the worst conditions I have ever sailed in. There were many times when I thought we would finish upside down,' he says of an event that cost one life, saw four yachts wrecked or rolled, and still sends shudders down his spine.

In the big races like the Whitbread where the competition is toughest, however, he has more often finished up the bridesmaid. 'He's never had lucky fingers,' said Cornelis van Rietschoten, the Dutch victor of the 1977/78 and 1981/82 Round The World Races. Lawrie Smith, skipper of the British Whitbread maxi *Rothmans*, entered in the 1989/90 race, described his New Zealand rival with greater bluntness: 'He's just not a winner and something will go wrong for him in this race too.'

But Blake and his 84ft ketch *Steinlager 2* proved them all wrong. He and his fourteen-strong crew dominated the 33,000-mile race from the outset, winning each stage to build up a one-and-a-half day lead over their compatriots aboard the rival New Zealand ketch *Fisher and Paykel*. No one else was ever in the frame.

For this fifth time round, he took the radical step of building the biggest, heaviest yacht in the race, fitted with a fractional ketch rig. Sailing in optimum conditions with the wind abeam, she carried twenty per cent more sail area than sloop-rigged rivals like *Rothmans* and proved to have a ten per cent speed average.

Even so, the Blake jinx struck at an early stage. The initial yacht built for the race had to be scrapped at the fitting-out stage after large areas of the high-tech carbonfibre moulded hull were found to have delaminated. It was only the goodwill of his sponsor, Lion-Nathan Breweries, which stumped up the immediate cash for another hull, that kept him in the race. The delay also cost him two months of vital preparation time and Blake must have wondered whether lightning could strike twice. Cautious not to tempt ill-luck, Blake said throughout this, his last Whitbread: 'The race is far from over. Anything can happen and I won't be counting chickens until after we cross the finish line in May.'

Yet it is this played-down attitude, coupled with his dogged determination, that had already made Blake a hero at home and a top international name. His skills as a seaman are on a level equal with fellow circumnavigators Eric Tabarly and Robin Knox-Johnston. His crew also held him in the highest regard and, for seven of them, this was the second or third time they have teamed up. Their reward was to be voted Sports Personalities of the Year mid-way through the 1989/90 race by the New Zealand media.

It was a following born as much from adversity and the public's love for the underdog as success. It began with *Ceramco*'s dismasting in the Atlantic just north of Ascension Island back in 1981. Lesser men would have turned on the engine and motored for the nearest port after seeing all hope of success crash down so early in the race for the second successive time. Instead, he motivated the crew to cannibalize the parts that remained to form a jury rig, and had the boat racing again within twenty-four hours.

The distance they had to cover was 2,455 miles, and they made what is now regarded as one of the epic voyages of modern times. Blake and his crew averaged close to 200-miles-a-day to reach Cape Town, the first stop-over, in time to rig a new mast and join the fleet for the start of the second stage to Auckland.

With nothing more to lose, they pushed their yacht to the limits, pressing the bigger Dutch entry *Flyer* throughout the remaining 20,000-mile voyage back to England. At Cape Horn, half an hour was all that divided them and, in the process, Blake and his boys won two of the remaining three legs on handicap. They also beat the previous best time for a fully-crewed circumnavigation, despite the time lost during the first stage of the

KZ-5555

Lion New Zealand, Peter Blake's entry in the fourth Whitbread, a heavy displacement maxi aboard which he finished second on elapsed time.

The pleasure of winning shows on the faces of Peter Blake and the crew of the big red Kiwi maxi. Opposite: the finish in sight for *Steinlager 2*.

navigation, despite the time lost during the first stage of the race. Back home, New Zealand's boating-mad population hung onto every word that came crackling across the air-waves, sharing each tense experience in a race that many were to compare with the latter-day classic between the two tea clippers *Thermopylae* and the *Cutty Sark* a century before.

The *Ceramco* campaign was sponsored by Sir Tom Clarke, then one of New Zealand's leading industrialists, together with three friends who helped to fund the sixty-eight-foot challenger. 'The crew were paid $2 a day in port and the total cost of the project was less than half that of *Steinlager 2*'s entire sail budget,' Blake recalls.

After a sailing career spent racing and delivering boats, Blake decided after the 1990 Whitbread that it was time to take up other opportunities – one of them to manage New Zealand's third America's Cup campaign.

Money has never been a motivation though Blake concedes now: 'Crews have never had it so good. When I began ocean racing with Robin Knox-Johnston and Leslie Williams, I paid for my share of the food onboard and the air tickets home.' Blake also remembers too well the disastrous preparations that cost them victory in the first two Whitbread races. 'In 1973, the start was our first sail on *Burton Cutter* and we were still fitting out the interior as we sailed down the English Channel. Even the heads (toilet) were not connected to the hull skin-fittings, and it took a week before we realised everything was going into the bilges,' he said. 'What Blake enjoys most is the adventure and camaraderie,' Peter Montgomery, the veteran New Zealand journalist who has followed Blake's every step, explained. 'He much preferred the days when it was your turn to be on deck if you couldn't play a hand of bridge.'

Life on racing yachts is not like that any more. Blake and his rivals pursued their Whitbread goals with the method and mentality required to win the America's Cup. Reminiscing over those early days of ill-preparation, Blake recalled: 'When we launched *Burton Cutter*, three tons of her lead ballast had been stolen and the boat was badly trimmed down by the bows. She needed four tons in the stern to get her to float on her marks. We told Alan Smith, her owner, who took the problem to his gun-smith saying he needed some lead shot. "Yes Sir, how many boxes?"

The reply astounded him as much as us, but he got the four tons of shot and we poured it into the skeg. When we set off in 1973, not only did we not have bunks, the seventy cases of beer had to be used as makeshift seats and there were no sheets for the sails. As we sailed off down the channel, there was a drum of rope in the cockpit and I cut them to size each time we hoisted a new sail.'

In another race, from Cape Town to Rio de Janeiro with Leslie Williams and Robin Knox-Johnston, aboard the first Ocean 71 *Ocean Spirit*, he was to learn all about victualling. 'Robin had invited gourmet Clement Freud as cook after a doctor had suggested he take a sea voyage. Freud arrived at Cape Town docks unannounced, wearing a boiler suit, and asked me "Well, where do you want it?" and tried to persuade me to take delivery of half a ton of coal!'

Freud's ideas on food requirements proved equally outlandish. 'Two large lorries arrived heaped full of all manner of luxury foods and good wines,' Peter recalls. 'When Robin saw it all stacked on the quayside, he went mad, and Clement was left crestfallen when the ingredients for half of his carefully worked out menus were sent back. Even so, we still had more than enough. Clement, then very disgruntled, stacked it away without envisaging that the boat might heel over, and after the first two tacks, everything had fallen out on the galley floor.'

Blake came back to join the pair aboard *Heath's Condor* to find, surprise, that the yacht's construction was far behind schedule. One misguided decision was to order an experimental 97ft carbon-fibre mast. 'It was so light, four of us could lift it easily. But it came without spreaders on the eve of the launch and two of us had to beg, borrow and steal enough lengths of mast section. We then grabbed a welder and worked through the night to fit it all together.' They were still working on the spreaders on the morning of the Whitbread start, and not surprisingly, the rig failed during the first leg.

Blake, whose byword now is preparation, is not easily caught out. He had done every job onboard and could perform them as well as any man on *Steinlager 2* – one reason why he became so revered by those who have worked under him. The *Steinlager 2* crew did get one over on him though during a pre-race shooting party in the Bay of Islands which he has never been able to forget. In an alcoholic chase for game in a Range Rover, the New Zealand skipper got out to open a gate, then shut it after the car had passed, leaving himself on the wrong side.

It caused considerable mirth, but one crewman who brought it up during a moment of chastisement paid dearly for it throughout the race. Blake put him on head-cleaning duties from day one and, according to another crewmate, he was forced to clean it so often during the race that his face became etched in the bowl!

Part Three

The 1993-94 Race

Chapter Six

The Course

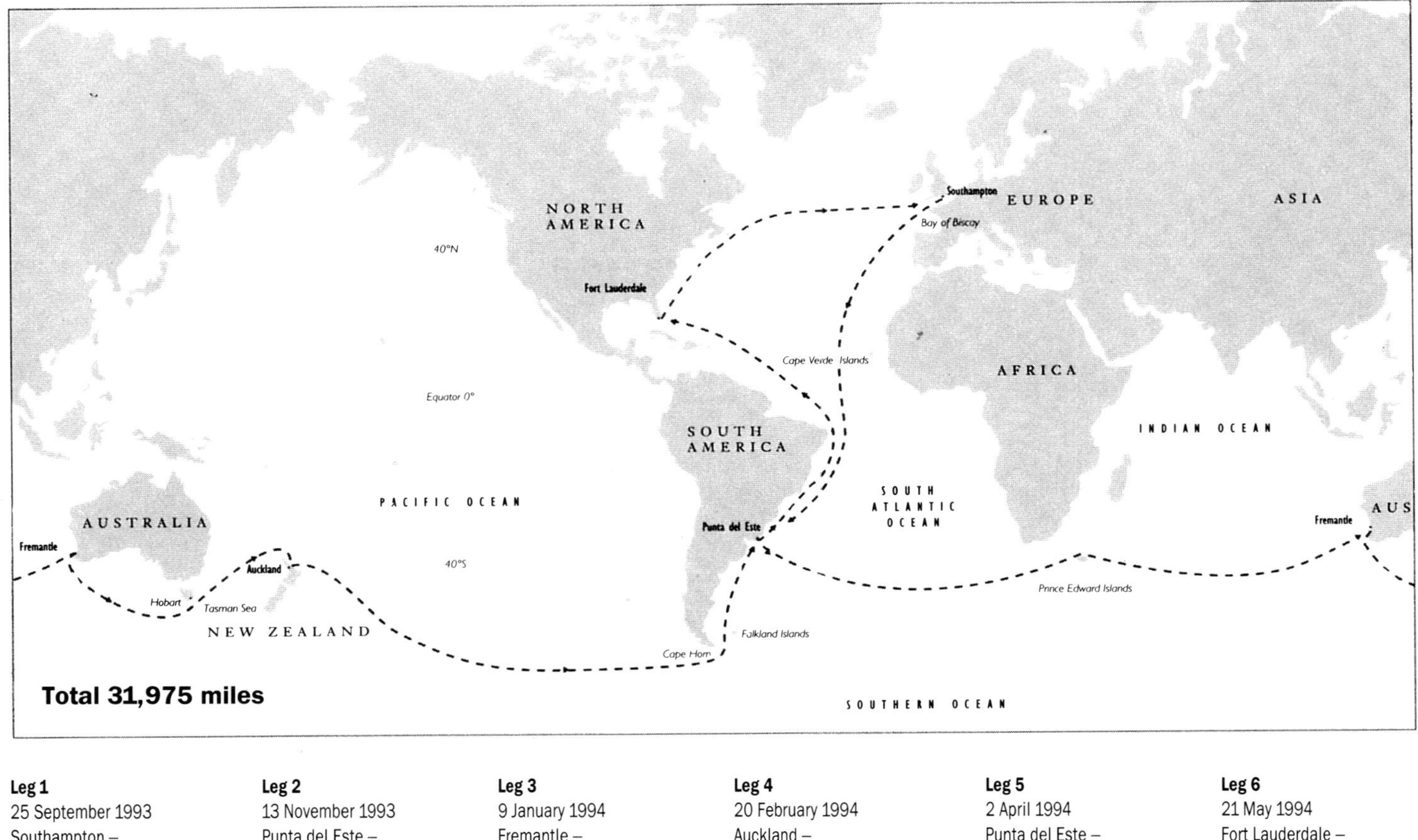

Leg 1	Leg 2	Leg 3	Leg 4	Leg 5	Leg 6
25 September 1993	13 November 1993	9 January 1994	20 February 1994	2 April 1994	21 May 1994
Southampton – Punta del Este (Uruguay)	Punta del Este – Fremantle (Australia)	Fremantle – Auckland (New Zealand)	Auckland – Punta del Este	Punta del Este – Fort Lauderdale (USA)	Fort Lauderdale – Southampton
5,938 nautical miles	7,558 nautical miles	3,272 nautical miles	5,914 nautical miles	5,475 nautical miles	3,818 nautical miles
	leaving Prince Edward Island to starboard	*leaving Tasmania to port*		*leaving the West Indies to port*	

Political and logistical reasons have forced changes to each successive Whitbread course. For the 1993 race, however, the difference is more subtle. For the first time the course skirts around Prince Edward Island, a natural bird sanctuary deep in the Roaring Forties, mid-way between the Uruguayan and Australian stop-overs.

The inclusion of this outcrop of rocks follows a controversial decision taken by the race organisers to reduce the risk of yachts running into ice during this long Southern Ocean stage south of the Indian Ocean after competitors in the 1989/90 experienced several 'near misses' in the fog.

Mercifully, no Whitbread yacht has ever hit an iceberg for there are no rescue services on standby that far south. Crews know that they are on their own and that, in the event of an emergency, they must rely in the short-term on chasing yachts providing assistance.

The first race in 1973/74 took in Cape Town, Sydney and Rio de Janeiro. That year, the event clashed with the annual Sydney/Hobart classic and the shortage of dock space led the RNSA to extend the Indian Ocean leg across the Tasman to Auckland, the 'City of Sails', for the next event four years later. The race has been to Auckland ever since, and sailing-mad New Zealanders have become renowned for providing the greatest welcomes and send-offs. The re-start now rivals the Solent start for the number of spectator boats shadowing the race yachts as they head out to sea.

After experiencing luke-warm receptions at Rio in 1974 and 1978, the third stop-over was moved south to the Argentine submarine port of Mar del Plata for the 1981/82 race. The aftermath of the Falklands War, however, forced the RNSA to seek another stop-over for the 1985/86 race and they moved across the River Plate to the Uruguayan resort of Punta del Este.

An outbreak of shootings and riots in the Cape townships during the 1985 stop-over in South Africa, and other political pressures, forced the RNSA to consider alternatives to the city they call the 'Tavern of the Seas'. Cape Town has been the natural stop-over for shipping ever since Vasco de Gama's fifteenth-century discovery of the Cape sea route to Asia, and the move away caused something of a dilemma.

The west African coastline is named the 'Skeleton Coast' for good reason but a move round to Mauritius in the Indian Ocean would have extended the first leg too far and taken the fleet outside the track of the southern ocean trades. In the end, the only solution was to re-draw the first leg across the Atlantic to Punta del Este and bring in Fremantle, Australia as a staging post to break up what would have been a 10,500-mile voyage to Auckland. As a result, Whitbread invested heavily into upgrading the infrastructure in Uruguay, providing the money for an operations annexe to be built at the Punta del Este Yacht Club, and donated a giant mobile hoist to lift the maxis out for repair at the docks in Montevideo. The port acted as a double stop-over during the 1989/90 race and will do so again during the sixth Whitbread, hosting the fleet at the end of the first and the fourth legs.

In 1990, for the first time, a North American port was included. Fort Lauderdale was chosen ahead of New York and Newport to widen US interest in the race. It also provided a final testing leg back to Britain which is to be retained for the 1993/4 event.

1993·94 WHITBREAD COURSE

Starting from the Solent at noon on 25 September 1993, the 5,938-mile opening leg to Punta del Este takes the fleet on a proving trial south across the Bay of Biscay and through the

As twilight begins to tint Punta del Este's high-rise buildings, *Drum*, skippered for the leg by the American veteran Skip Novak, finishes the first leg.

north east trade-wind belt to the Doldrums, the first tactical test.

This roulette wheel of calms spanning the Atlantic just north of the Equator can trap yachts for anything between six hours and six days. The area is best likened to a pot of boiling water, for the upward movement of air bubbles is so indiscriminate that the wind is impossible to forecast.

These calms, which vary between 10 degrees and 18 degrees N, are controlled by two high-pressure systems to the north and south. It is the air from these systems converging erratically into the Doldrums, that rise up into cells of cumulonimbus cloud before condensing to create the rainstorms that can provide such welcome relief. Any crew that can break clear of the fleet here can expect an uninterrupted run through the south east trades to Punta del Este and gain a considerable jump on the fleet.

The inclusion of Prince Edward Island as a mark of the course mid-way through the 7,558-mile second stage to Fremantle provides an interesting problem for crews. During previous races, navigators have had to balance the shorter distance of the great circle route (approx 60 degrees S) against the extreme cold, the threat of ice and strong possibility of running into unfavourable headwinds.

The strong winds are generated by two sets of low-pressure systems traversing the Southern Ocean in an easterly direction. The centre of the larger of these skirts the icy wastes of Antarctica around 60 degrees S, while the smaller, faster-moving secondary lows flow around the glove further north. It is these more vigorous systems that, uninterrupted by land, create the very strong winds in the aptly named Roaring Forties and Furious Fifties latitudes.

As with all lows in the Southern Ocean, these circulate clockwise, providing strong reaching and running westerly winds for yachts north of their centres – and adverse headwinds for any caught to the south.

Those crews finding themselves on the wrong side of a low during past races have always returned with chilling tales. During the 1981 race, the New Zealand yacht *Outward Bound* went down as far as 62 degrees S only to find that sails and control lines became so stiff with ice that it is impossible to reef. 'It was more like skiing than sailing down there,' skipper Digby Taylor said in Auckland. 'Lifelines became encrusted with ice two inches thick, winches could only be freed by pouring hot water over them and our sails were always full of snow.'

Two Scandinavian entries, *Berge Viking* and *Swedish Entry* went even lower – to 66 degrees S – where conditions became so cold that breaking water froze instantly on deck. 'We had icebergs all around us,' said *Viking*'s skipper Peter Lunde. 'It was just impossible to sail the boat hard or set a spinnaker with the worry of all that ice about.'

For those who judge it right, this leg, like the fourth stage to Cape Horn, will turn into an exciting roller-coaster ride as the yachts surge across the Southern Ocean in a series of 350-plus-mile days. Arriving at Fremantle in mid-December, the crews take a break to enjoy Christmas in the sun before departing on the 3,272-mile third stage to Auckland on 9 January 1994.

This is a fairly simple leg in terms of weather. The yachts take the great circle route, just skirting Tasmania, before heading north east across the Tasman Sea for Cape Reinga, New Zealand's northern-most point, and turning south for the final 200-mile run to Auckland.

Crews could well enjoy a second bite of the Southern Ocean during the dive south of Australia, but the principal danger during past races has been collisions with whales migrating through the Tasman Sea. *Lion New Zealand*, Peter Blake's entry in the 1985/86 race, lost the greater part of her rudder after ramming into one of these basking mammals and *Charles Jourdan*, Alain Gabbay's entry in the 1989/90 circumnavigation

Damage caused by a whale strike to *Charles Jourdan* proving that weather is not the only opponent on the high seas. Opposite: *Steinlager 2* at the Needles when only a dismasting could prevent her winning the leg and with it the race.

came off decidely second-best when hitting a whale in almost exactly the same position.

The next 5,914-mile stage back to Punta del Este provides the challenge that most crews enter this race for – Cape Horn.

The yachts will dive south immediately after leaving Auckland in an effort to hit the Roaring Forties first, then sweep eastwards on a composite great circle route, well inside the ice limits, before rounding the infamous Cape and heading north between the Falkland Islands and mainland.

The weather guidelines for the south Indian Ocean also hold true for the South Pacific. Crews must avoid crossing south of the low pressure systems, especially as they close on the Horn, as this would otherwise leave them beating into some of the harshest conditions in the world.

During both the 1981/82 race and the last Whitbread circumnavigation, some crews were disappointed to find themselves in flat calm. That was unusual, for the weather is almost always bad, blowing a full gale most days, and stormy the rest, building up to hurricane force on an average of twelve days a year.

Once north, crews will want to avoid the adverse Falklands current by keeping well east of the 100-fathom line which also provides a windward advantage for the final track into Punta del Este.

The 5,475-mile fifth stage northwards to Fort Lauderdale starting on 2 April proved something of a Caribbean cruise during the last race. Lawrie Smith and this *Rothmans'* crew stole a march on their rivals during the initial stages by keeping well east of the adverse Brazil current sweeping down the South American coast, but the fleet closed up again close to the Equator when the Doldrums took their wind. Thereafter, the race degenerated into a procession through to the Florida finish.

By contrast the final 3,818-mile stage back to Southampton, starting from Fort Lauderdale on 21 May could provide a nail-biting finale judging by the history of the last race when the first two yachts finished within thirty-six minutes of each other back at Southampton and the fourth boat was home within twelve hours.

The course is a simple great circle route across the Atlantic, for crews who stray further north are penalised with a sudden drop in temperatures and the prospects of head winds and fog as they cross the Newfoundland Banks.

Closer to home, the weather in the English Channel is rarely the same two days in succession. Crews are just as likely to experience a south westerly gale as easterly headwinds, but either is likely to provide a tense climax to this 33,000-mile race.

Previous pages: ski goggles for spray protection are obligatory for the first Russian crew aboard *Fazisi*, seen here battling against the elements.

Chapter Seven

The Whitbread 60-footer

***Yamaha*, Ross Field's Farr-designed Whitbread 60, the first boat built to the new rule. Opposite: *Brooksfield*, the second 60-footer. The new class promises to combine the speed of the old maxis, without the exorbitant costs.**

The Whitbread 60 Rule was developed not only to satisfy those searching for an exciting new yacht to challenge the oceans of the world, but also as a defence against a move by the Offshore Maxi Yacht Association (OMYA) to take over the race. It had for a long time been patently obvious that the IOR was not the best way to handicap the wide variety of boats in this race. They had become too disparate in size for the long-accepted rule to be able to cope with any degree of fairness and while the maxi-raters had, at last, begun to race on level terms, there was no similarly accepted standard for other boats.

OMYA's members suggested that a separate class be formed, which it saw as a 'starter' division from which competitors could 'graduate' to the maxis. The proposal was for a 60ft one-design, which would be to general IOR principals, designed by Bruce Farr. Whitbread was expected to fund the design and would jointly share the royalties from each boat built with OMYA. Thus the maxi-owners would have a source of income to keep their operation solvent and, at the same time, be responsible for administering the smaller class of boat. The one-design would have to be decidely slower than the maxis – a very definite second-class option in the race (OMYA stated that it 'will not support any proposal for a one-off class unless it has . . . an arrival date two to three days after the maxis'). The flaws in this proposed system were all too obvious.

It was thus, at a cocktail party in Uruguay at the second stop-over of the 1989/90 race, that Bob Fisher approached David Pritchard-Barrett and John Anson, Whitbread's race and finance directors respectively, with an alternative suggestion. It was that Whitbread should fund a rule formulation project for a class for the next race; and that this rule might be extended to provide other levels for non-handicap racing, from twenty-five to fifty feet in five-foot increments for other events. The proposal

I
12555
I-12555
Brooksfield
I-12555
Brooksfield

Deprived of her water ballast, *Yamaha* ships a huge crew for the Kenwood Race. In the Whitbread she will rely on ballast, not bodies, to achieve added stability.

found some immediate interest and Fisher was requested to provide a detailed paper on the subject so that the Whitbread board might consider its viability. This done, a meeting of skippers and others proposing to take part in the next race was called for the next race stop-over in Fort Lauderdale.

The meeting was presented with a paper written by Rob Humphreys and Fisher, giving the alternatives available, even to a major rethinking and reworking of the IOR so that, to use Humphreys' own words, 'we should not throw out the baby with the bathwater.' In reply, there were those who wanted a 'box' rule, one in which only the basic parameters would be defined; others wanted to adopt the few parameters used by the boats which race in the BOC Single-handed Race.

What was required was a rule which would give yacht designers some room for manoeuvre but, at the same time, instantly produce a class in which the racing would be close in all weather conditions. The boats had to have some construction restrictions to make them less expensive, relatively, than the maxis where, between races, all-out technological warfare had more than doubled their cost.

The new America's Cup class rule formulation had pointed to the way in which the operation might be successful and all the lessons learned from that operation – good and bad – were observed in setting up the organisation for the Whitbread 60 Rule. A three-day conference was convened, at Goodwood, to which the leading racing-yacht designers were invited together with construction experts and a leavening of rule-makers.

The design conference was held at the beginning of June 1990 with a brief that the rule had to be available for presentation to competitors at a meeting held at the London Boat Show at the beginning of January 1991. It was a formidable project but the progress made at the three-day conference put the entire operation into perspective and gave admirable direction to the group which was subsequently formed to process the deliberations.

The Whitbread Offshore Rule had to produce boats which were faster, safer, more exciting to sail and less expensive than their IOR counterparts. It was to be a totally new rule, one which did not intend to rate existing boats or provide the basis for handicaps; rather, to produce level rating yachts to the differing ideas of various designers. It had to be 'type forming' so that the boats from a variety of designers thoughts were to turn out to sail at very much the same speed.

The conference divided into groups to deal with various aspects of the rule – length management, rig, water ballast and construction among them. Perhaps the trickiest point was that of length. It is generally understood that the length of a boat is a controlling factor in its maximum hull speed. That 'length' is not overall or waterline but the 'sailing length' which includes part of its forward and aft overhangs. Therefore much of the effort of this group, under the leadership of David Pedrick, was devoted to defining this length. The forward and aft overhang components are calculated from the measurement of two forward and two aft girths and from these an intersection of the component lines with a defined waterplane establishes the 'sailing length,' L. In basic terms, more girth aft would require a reduced static waterline length, while the bow girths control the rake of the stem – this is also restricted to a maximum of thirty-five degrees from the vertical. It was decided that all measurements should be taken out of the water and then floatation marks be impressed in the hull. The boat is then floated and ballasted, if necessary, until she sits at those marks in measurement condition in a manner similar to that employed in the metre-boat classes for many years. It is a system in which sailors have confidence. Since the only acceptable method of determining the displacement of a yacht is to weigh it, it was decided that modern loadcells accurate to within 50kg in 20 tonnes could adequately provide the correct information and all boats built to the rule would therefore have to be weighed.

The rig is almost one-design with predetermined maximum heights of the mast and foretriangle. The base of the foretriangle also has a defined maximum measurement as have the spinnaker leech and bowsprit lengths. Every encouragement is given to rigs without overlapping headsails so that the shrouds can be taken to chainplates on the hull shell, rather than inboard, which provides a stronger staying base for the rig. Fully-battened mainsails, with girth controls to limit the roach, were considered efficient; the rule limiting roach is so that mainsails will clear the mandatory standing backstay. Masthead spinnakers and drifters were very much part of the philosophy of the rule but the use of these sails has been restricted by the RNSA in order to preserve the 'premium quality' of the maxis. The rule was seen to have been capable of producing sixty-footers capable of beating the eighty-five-foot maxis.

Water ballast was always considered as a viable speed-producing factor to be encouraged. It is limited by tanks of no more than 5,000 litres capacity. Water is also the racing sailors' enemy and much thought was given to the safety of the Whitbread 60 class with a demand for the hull to be divided into at least four watertight compartments, excluding the tankage, by watertight bulkheads, two forward and one aft. There is, in the rule, a requirement for the minimum height of the deck above the water with any one of the compartments flooded.

All-in-all, the final rule meets all the policy requirements. It produces fast, sloop-rigged monohulls of similar performance, suitable for long distance racing offshore at the highest level of the sport. The need for safety is paramount and the rule is intended to foster design developments leading to easily-driven, seaworthy yachts of high stability, requiring moderate crew numbers. Yachting columnist Andrew Preece described the impact of the rule as giving a new focus to the race. 'It has centred the attention away from the maxis.' he said. He believes that it will put the deciding factor of the race increasingly on the people rather than the boats which they sail. He feels that it is a possibility that the 60s may beat the maxis on certain legs, but points to the performance of the light-displacement boats on the 1989/90 race where they produced some prodigious daily runs but were unable to sustain high speeds over an entire leg. 'It will also depend on whether they (the race committee) slow them down any more.'

W60
1
YAMAHA

Chapter Eight

Speed

Steinlager 2 **– 128 days 9 hours for the six-leg 1989/90 race. Opposite:** ***GB II*** **– 144 days 11 hours in 1973 and 134 days 12 hours in 1977 for the four-leg race. Overleaf;** ***Fortuna Extra Lights*** **– 403 miles in twenty-four hours.**

Speed is king, within the limits of safety, but there is little doubt that in succeeding races, the sailors have been prepared to push their charges harder and harder. Speeds have progressively risen, a combination of better boats and increasing skills; better boats because their added speed potential had made them inherently safer, and better handling has allowed them to sail faster. It is little wonder, therefore, that the speed of the fastest boat has increased from the 7.77 knots of *Great Britain II* in 1973/74 to 10.68 of *Steinlager 2* in 1989/90 – thirty-seven per cent faster.

There is no doubt that the crew of *Great Britain II* were on a steep learning-curve in that first race and might easily have sailed her faster. The paratroopers had not had a great deal of experience with the seventy-seven-footer before the race began and while the same could be said of her crew the next time around, the vast amount of miles that Rob James had sailed in her undoubtedly improved her performance – her average speed in the 1977/78 race was 8.35 knots.

The speeds of the slowest yachts in the race also give some idea of the general progression of the race. In 1973/74, the Polish forty-five-footer, *Copernicus*, took the greatest time, nearly 205 days for the 26,950 miles, an average of 5.48 knots – sixteen years later, the longest time taken by any of the yachts in the race was the 182 days of the 51ft *La Poste* for a total distance of 32,926 miles at 7.54 knots, again thirty-seven per cent faster.

Yachts in that first race were hardly of the grand prix type, even as it was then considered. Some were old and only a few had been built specifically for the job. The older ones included boats built of steel and wood but the major material used was good old-fashioned glassfibre, and old-fashioned was the best possible description. Only the three biggest boats –

K
3566
GREAT BRITAIN II
RAMSGATE

E 1992
Fortuna
E
1992
Fortuna

Fortuna

***Pen Duick VI*, Eric Tabarly's André Mauric-designed ketch which gained extra stability from a spent uranium keel. Opposite: note *King's Legend*'s winch pedestal.**

Burton Cutter, *Pen Duick VI* and *Great Britain II* – were built with any real thought of utilising modern materials; the first two in aluminium and Chay Blyth's Alan Gurney design of glassfibre.

Burton Cutter suffered from engineering problems in her construction and had to be virtually rebuilt after encountering big seas early on the second leg. *Pen Duick* was so strong that she twice lost her mainmast and *Great Britain II* was built while glassfibre technicians were groping in the dark. The foam between the two layers of glassfibre was known to have absorbed a great deal of water (and with that, weight) although the boat continued to hold together through six round-the-world races. By the standards of the early 1990s, they were still extremely heavily-built and the old maxim of Uffa Fox does hold true, that 'weight is only of value in a steamroller.'

Lighter boats are faster, particularly downwind, where most of the Whitbread Race is held and, to some extent, the fifth Whitbread was held with a greater proportion of downwind sailing than its predecessors. It wasn't until the second race that anyone seriously examined weight or even contemplated the advantages of different rigs. The indications were, from some research, that a sloop was more efficient than a ketch. *King's Legend*, the only sloop-rigged Swan 65 in the 1977/78 race was easily able to hold off her ketch-rigged sisterships and that did more to promote the security which many felt in the choice of the single-masted rig that was to persist in Pierre Fehlmann, for instance, right up to the end of the fourth leg of the 1989/90 race. Conny van Rietschoten chose a ketch rig deliberately for *Flyer* in 1977 and he explained the choice as a means of getting better speed out of the boat in reaching conditions. Wrote van Rielschoten:

'A ketch rig was chosen to give a wide variety of sail combinations and in order that no sails would be too large for one watch to handle on their own. *Flyer* was drawn with a larger mizzen than those on the ketch-rigged Swan 65s, to improve reaching and downwind performance. *Flyer* showed her best speeds when close reaching, and on all points of sailing in strong winds. The only time *Flyer* gave away speed to the sloop-rigged Swan 65 *King's Legend* was in light airs, either sailing close hauled or going dead downwind, where she proved to be undercanvassed.

Olin Stephens had specified short length spreaders for his mizzen-mast; the shrouds ran to inboard chainplates on the deck and the reduced effective angle was compensated for by a heavier mast section. The rig allowed the mizzen genoa to be set with as little as sixty degrees apparent wind angle on the instruments. This sail could be used to good effect in anything up to force five and when set would immediately add a knot to boatspeed. It was a real advantage to us in light conditions like these and when carrying it *Flyer* would often outpace the sloop-rigged *King's Legend* by fifteen to twenty miles a day. This was our secret weapon and was to pay handsome dividends.

Weight, however, was an even bigger consideration then and after the second race. Butch Dalrymple-Smith, who became a partner in the Ron Holland design office after crewing *Sayula II* in the first race, was to contribute this short treatise on construction techniques to van Rietschoten's book.

'The structural design of a sailing yacht is treated as an inexact science or an extremely tedious business. Even using the most sophisticated finite-element model computer analysis, the calculation of a boat as a statistically indeterminate structure is a long process. It is hardly surprising, therefore, that the majority of design offices still use precedent and extrapolation to calculate the scantlings for their boats. But if designers are to make the most of hi-tech composite materials then a computer analysis of the hull loadings is essential.

Although displacement and vertical centre of gravity are

27-10-77
NOVAK. QUOTE
"I REALY LIKE
THE SOUTHERN
OCEAN"

This is what Whitbread crews seek from the race – giant downhill slides on the waves of the Southern Ocean. However many times they do it, the sensation is new.

***Steinlager 2* under construction in Auckland in near laboratory conditions. The giant hull showing carbon laminate prior to final skinning. Opposite: *Flyer*, until *Steinlager 2*, the most convincing Whitbread winner.**

taken into account when measuring a yacht under IOR, there is a considerable speed advantage to be gained by concentrating the weight in the centre of the boat. This encourages designers to reduce the structural weight to a minimum and convert it into ballast which, placed closer to the centre of pitching, reduces the tendency for the boat to dig into a wave before rising and lifting over it. On the other hand, it is also essential for the hull to be puncture resistant, provide a rigid base for the rig, and exhibit sufficient panel stiffness to prevent flexing under hydrodynamic pressure which absorbs energy from the waves and hurts boatspeed.'

At that time, aluminium was the favoured material for racing boats over forty feet long, but to be effective it required a complex structure of frames and stringers within the hull. Thin plating was difficult to weld without distortion and, to get round the disadvantages, glue and rivet techniques, first pioneered in the aircraft industry, found their way into boatbuilding, at least for smaller boats. The conventional aluminium building of larger boats continued, which had the added advantage of being easy to repair and to modify, thereby extending the competitive life of a boat. It was not, however, perfect as Butch Dalrymple-Smith explains: 'Sandwich construction provides the best building medium. As far as stiffness is concerned there is no substitute for thickness, and by utilizing a low density core material, weight can be carefully controlled.'

When van Rietschoten planned the second *Flyer* for the 1981/82 race, he took the aluminium route as the composite constructional engineering of a maxi was insufficiently researched and the designer, German Frers, was in constant liaison with Wolter Huisman and his boatyard at Vollenhove in Holland over the construction of *Helisara VI* for Herbert von Karajan. Van

***UBS*, a composite constructed boat with an aluminium sub frame to take the major loads. Opposite: *Satquote British Defender* with a few miles to go to Fremantle.**

Rietschoten had seen the lines of *Helisara VI* and considered them correct for his purpose. The design was a development of *Bumblebee 4*, which had taken line honours in the 1979 Sydney-Hobart and followed that with a similar victory in the next year's Bermuda Race prior to winning the Maxi World Championship.

There were, necessarily, some minor alterations to be made to what was essentially an inshore maxi design to make it suitable for the Whitbread. The balanced rudder gave way to a skeg-hung one as a protection against collision with underwater objects and the transom slope was increased to make it 'easier for the crew to perform their natural functions over the stern.'

One area in which van Rietschoten, aiming solely for line honours and a record time, was frustrated was in not being able to install a ketch rig. The extra engineering would have put the boat behind schedule and those around him did their best to convince him that a sloop would be better. He might have been swayed to a composite construction had he known what the Holland-designed *Kialoa IV*'s hull and deck mouldings weighed – 6,500lb compared with the calculation of 9,500lb had it been built in aluminium.

Since that race, there have been huge gains in constructional engineering to gain fractions of a knot in speed. Hulls of carbon-fibre laminates, pre-impregnated with epoxy resins, baked in an autoclave are now *de rigeur*. The differences that can be made are minimal but the small differences between the boats at the end of each leg necessitate the recourse to high-tech building and all its additional expense. Neither Lawrie Smith nor Pierre Fehlmann would have wanted anything but the very best when they were engaged in their nail-biting finish to the second leg of the 1989/90 race at Fremantle.

The only comparisons of speed that Whitbread boats can be subjected to are to those of other performances in the same race. Even other Whitbread races are hardly fair as the 'pitch' is not level. Different weather conditions make for very different speed potentials. When *Flyer* raised the average speed for the race to 9.35 knots in 1981/82 by going round the course in fourteen days less then *Great Britain II* four years earlier, it was in regular Southern Ocean weather. That Pierre Fehlmann's *UBS Switzerland* was only two-and-a-half days quicker for a speed increase of 0.22 knots was due to the softer reaching winds rather than the full-blasting square-running conditions normally found in the Southern Ocean.

By then, however, speeds were already high and the increases might be expected to be small but when *Steinlager 2* went round the extended course 10.5 per cent faster than *UBS* had done, there were some obvious reasons for it. As van Rietschoten had proved to himself, the ketch rig has a speed advantage; it is also advantaged under the IOR and will be used by every serious skipper in the 1993/94 race.

What has also improved is the technology of sails, not only in the materials used but also in their engineering. Some of it has come in spin-offs from the America's Cup, notably in the design of gennakers but also in the construction of fore-and-aft sails. Kevlar only proliferated through the Whitbread fleet in the fourth race, despite its use in shorter races, as it was believed to be more suspect to ultraviolet light failure than was true.

Sail engineering has led to considerable reductions in weight. The research into stress patterns has given sailmakers the opportunity to contribute tremendously to the speed potential of Whitbread racing yachts in several areas, and the research for the marathon races has benefited the average sailor. Sails specially laminated using monofilament threads laid to the stress patterns by the Sobstad organisation were used by *Satquote British Defender* in the 1989/90 race and, using polyester threads rather than Kevlar, have found their way aboard cruising boats. The gennakers which were used on the mizzens of the ketches, themselves derived from America's Cup boats, are forerunners of the modern cruising chutes.

The speed of *Steinlager 2* was high compared with that of most ocean racers although the record for a race is held by the ultra-light 67ft *Pied Piper* over the 333-mile Chicago-Mackinac race in 1987. *Pied Piper* averaged 12.88 knots but over a relatively short distance. In Whitbread terms, this is easily eclipsed by the performance of *Fortuna Extra Lights* which in one noon-to-noon run covered 398 miles at an average of 16.58 knots. On three other occasions, in twenty-four hours, not noon-to-noon, the same yacht covered over 400 miles, her best being 403 miles for 16.79 knots. On the leg she achieved these remarkable performances, *Fortuna Extra Lights* only averaged 11.3 knots (*Steinlager 2* averaged 11.7 knots), which shows how hard it is to maintain high averages for a long period of time.

Purely for comparison, the best monohull ocean record is that of the four-masted, 244ft schooner *Phocea*, which crossed the North Atlantic at an average speed of 14.96 knots. The speeds of multihulls are higher still with the same North Atlantic crossing, by *Jet Services V* in 1990 at 18.62 knots. The following year, Florence Arthaud in the 458-mile Marseilles to Carthage race averaged 20.66 knots and Thierry Bielak achieved 44.66 knots over a 500-metre course on a sailboard.

R.N.S.A.
R.A.F.S.A.
BRITISH
DEFENDER

Chapter Nine

Satellite Communications

It was back in the 1970s that live man's first tentative steps on the moon were witnessed live on television. The video telephone was first demonstrated in the 1980s. Surprisingly, it is only in the 1990s that it has become possible to capture live the excitement and dangers aboard yachts racing far out on the ocean waves.

In past Whitbread races, crews reaching port after sailing 7,000 miles across the barren wastes of the Southern Ocean have talked endlessly of roller-coaster rides down towering white crested waves, of collisions with whales and of running an almost endless gauntlet between fog-shrouded icebergs. Now, thanks to some pioneering technology developed by BT (formerly British Telecom) the rest of the world can witness the dramas almost as soon as they occur during the 1993/94 race.

The problems that had to be overcome were considerable. First there was the little matter of linking up with a satellite from a badly pitching deck. Then there was the problem of the limited power source available on a yacht. Both were overcome with the miniaturization of the Inmarsat-A onboard transmitter. One version of this mushroom shaped equipment, which is steadied by a gyro, is small enough to be sited under the deck and proved its worth and reliability aboard Ludde Ingvall's *UBF Finland* during the 1989/90 race when the system was used as a simple data/voice transmitter. The biggest breakthrough however, came with the advances made in video 'phone technology and the use of digital compression techniques that reduce the signals required to produce a recognisable picture down to a manageable number for transmission down a simple 9.6k/bit telephone line. 'It is not the technology so much as the limited pathway of the telephone and the power available on a yacht that restricts us;' Edward Scott from BT explained when the first tests were carried out aboard the former Whitbread yacht *Rothmans* during the 1991 Fastnet race.

The problems have been overcome in part by the compression system fitted onboard the yachts in this latest race. This scans each picture grouping the outline and colours into a series of digital codes, which are then translated back into picture form at BT's Telecom Tower in London ready for onward transmission to television stations around the world.

It is possible to send live pictures back from the boats, but the quality is enhanced to a more acceptable level with what BT call their 'store-and-forward' transmission techniques. 'It's rather like an egg timer with the sand transferred from top to bottom over an extended period without change of form or volume. In our system, the bottle neck is the 64kbit/sec Inmarsat-A satellite link,' Scott explained. 'The more signals we can send through, the better the picture. As a result, a two-minute clip edited onboard the yacht takes between twelve and twenty-four minutes to transmit.'

The quality is still noticeably lower than film footage transmitted over a land link, but nevertheless, the development is seen as a significant breakthrough by television producers like Gary Lovejoy, the head of sport at Independent Television News who leads the international television pool for Whitbread race coverage. 'For the first time, we can carry live bulletins during each leg instead of relying on library footage for the month these yachts take to get from one port to another. It is certain to bring the race alive.' he says. The Inmarsat-A system weights 150kg and though it is not compulsory for yachts to carry it, the race rules insist that compensating weights must be fitted onboard yachts without the satellite transmitter. BT has also tailored the Inmarsat-C data system to plot and track the fleet as it races around the world. The C-Sat equipment which weighs only a few kilograms and is compulsory onboard each yacht, combines this latest satellite data transmission system with the American global positioning system (GPS). This allows the race organisers to call up each yacht, a group or the entire fleet at any time to check their positions with pin-point accuracy. This means that close-fought duels become watchable 'minute-by-minute' via BT's computer graphic display, and checks can be made that yachts actually round marks of the course such as Prince Edward Island deep in the Indian Ocean. The system, which was used for the first time during the 1992/3 British Steel Challenge round the world race, can also be accessed by the general public who can poll charts showing the course and position of each yacht on a fax machine. It proved so effective during the British Steel race that the BT system was called on to deal with up to 200 calls an hour – a number that is likely to increase with calls from all around the world during the 1993/94 Whitbread.

BT's C-Sat system, which has been developed to track anything from ships to a fleet of vehicles around the globe, also has a number of safety features. A panic button allows crews to alert the race organisers and rescue authorities the moment an emergency arises. If there is time before abandoning ship, a crew can also spell out the nature of their problem by selecting one of a number of scenarios from a menu displayed on the computer. All told, these developments mark a significant step forward from the ageing Argos system which, as Chay Blyth found when he capsized off Cape Horn, can take up to nineteen hours to alert the rescue authorities.

STC
STR 9120

Chapter Ten

The 1993-94 Entrants

New Zealand Endeavour, one of three new maxis designed by Bruce Farr for the 1993-94 race.

When this chapter was written in March 1993, nine new boats, purpose-built for the Whitbread had already been launched and eight were under construction. This high level of new boats was largely due to the Whitbread 60 class, which was introduced to create boats not only more suited to the Southern Ocean, but also more suited to a sponsor's budget. The twelve syndicates which had formally entered in March are featured opposite and overleaf; here we outline those which, although not entered, are deep in preparation for the race.

Principal among these is the UK-based project for disabled sailors *Dolphin W60*. The brainchild of polio-victim Brendan Foley, the project has built a W60 to a Rob Humphreys design and has been training extensively. The crew will feature sailors who have overcome some form of disability.

Matthew Humphries who, at 18, was the youngest crew member in the last race, heads The Youth Challenge, a project which hopes to find support to enter an existing maxi.

Following the media and sailing success of the all-women team on *Maiden* it is surprising that the opportunity to sponsor another women's entry has not been taken up but, so far, neither an American-based team nor a European team has managed to find the whole budget.

It is expected that many of the maxis that raced in the 1989-90 Whitbread will be entered again. Giorgio Falck, the Italian who has entered three Whitbreads, owns the 1989-90 winner *Steinlager 2* and a Spanish group led by Jan Santana own the second-placed *Fisher & Paykel*. Both are likely to be in the Race. Uruguay will have its first entry if sponsorship is found for *Uruguay Natural*, formerly *Martela OF*. An American group, ORCA, are also planning to enter a maxi whose campaign will be used as an educational and inspirational tool in American schools. There may also be several new Russian maxis, all built, of course, at former aerospace factories!

The 1993-94 Whitbread Round The World Race has already attracted a record number of enquiries and of these nearly 100 are registered with the Race Office. Most of them have yet to discover that the hardest part of the race is not dodging icebergs in the Southern Ocean nor finding wind in the Doldrums, it is securing sponsorship. Having tried and failed, the start of the race will be a poignant day for them.

MAXIS

Boat: La Poste

Flag: France
Skipper: Daniel Mallé
Designer: Bruce Farr

La Poste represents the French Post Office's second foray into the Whitbread. La Poste entered the 1989-90 race with the smallest boat in the fleet, a Bénéteau 51, crewed entirely by postal workers. Despite never being able to keep up with her larger rivals, *La Poste* captured the admiration of the fleet and the imagination of postal workers everywhere.

The project was such a success that the French Post Office decided to enter again, but this time with a competitive boat. The new *La Poste* was launched on 6 February, 1993 in Port Camargue, France.

Designed by the giant of IOR designers, Bruce Farr, the new maxi is about as similar to the old *La Poste* as a motor launch to a rubber dinghy. It is long, sleek and has the distinctive and, at the time, controversial clipper bow, of her Farr-designed sister ships.

La Poste will again have a postman, Daniel Mallé, as skipper, but only half of the crew will be postmen. The remainder are America's Cup sailors, Olympic medallists and Whitbread sailors. Mallé explained: 'I have taken some like my second in command, Benoît Caignaert, who comes from offshore racing and the America's Cup, and also those who know the Southern Ocean like João Cabeçadas, who was navigator for Patrick Tabarly in the last race.'

Other key members of the crew are 1992 Figaro winner Michel Desjoyeaux and navigator Dominique Conin.

Boat: New Zealand Endeavour

Flag: New Zealand
Skipper: Grant Dalton
Designer: Bruce Farr

New Zealander Grant Dalton spent the last Whitbread chasing his compatriot and rival Peter Blake, finishing a valiant second to *Steinlager 2*'s emphatic first. It is an experience Dalton does not wish to repeat. 'Coming second is not good enough – I of all people understand that,' said Dalton. 'When you set a goal and don't quite reach it, you can't just set it aside; you can't be satisfied, you can't say "the end".'

This single-minded determination has been applied to every aspect of the campaign. His Farr-designed maxi was launched in November 1992 and for her ocean-racing debut won line honours in the 650-mile Sydney to Hobart Race.

New Zealand Endeavour is built from carbon fibre and is lighter than her predecessor *Fisher & Paykel*. Even the interior was left unpainted to save 100kg of weight. Her mizzen mast is nearly as high as the main mast and is set well back to make better use of the all-important staysails. The developments are working as Dalton says the boat is faster than *Fisher & Paykel*.

Dalton had a deep pool of New Zealand talent from which to choose his crew. On his fourth Whitbread himself, Dalton has chosen Whitbread veterans Murray Ross (navigator), Kevin Shoebridge, Glen Sowry, Allan Prior, Tony Rae, Craig Watson and Cole Sheehan for key positions.

Boat: Merit Cup

Flag: Switzerland
Skipper: Pierre Fehlmann
Designer: Bruce Farr

Pierre Fehlmann is equally determined to win the next Whitbread, having tasted victory before. His was the fastest boat in the 1985-86 Whitbread but did not win on handicap. He returned in 1989-90 determined to win both prizes, but made the error of choosing to stay with a sloop rig, rather than try the new-style ketch rig. He was never able to match the boat speed of the Kiwi ketches and had to be satisfied with third.

Immediately after the 1989-90 Race he had *Merit* converted to a ketch to learn how to get the most from the rig and commissioned a new ketch-rigged maxi from Bruce Farr. *Merit Cup* is the exact sistership of *La Poste* as the two syndicates decided to share the all-important research before the design was finalised. They even shared builders and will train together in the build-up to the race.

Their design does not appear to be substantially different from *New Zealand Endeavour* – which should make crew and tactics the winning factors.

Fehlmann is one of the few who can truly claim to be a full-time professional Whitbread skipper. He raced his first Whitbread, as a skipper, in 1977 and has been 'offshore' ever since. His recipe for a winning crew is to have an afterguard of trusted Whitbread veterans leading a new crew of 'hungry' sailors on their first Whitbread. Fehlmann's afterguard for 1993 are: Gerard Rogivue, Nicolas Berthoud, André Loepfe and George Wagner.

The new crew was selected and trained during the three years of the OMYA series between Whitbreads. This time on the water for the crew is something that *La Poste* shares but *New Zealand Endeavour* does not.

Boat: Fortuna

Flag: Spain
Skipper: Lawrie Smith
Designer: Javier Visiers

As an ultra-light displacement sloop in the 1989-90 Whitbread, *Fortuna Extra Lights* achieved daily runs of over 400 nautical miles in the heavy winds of the Southern Ocean, but did not excel in the light winds that prevailed at the beginning and end of each leg. To improve on this performance the designer and project manager, Javier Visiers, had the yacht chain-sawed in half and added 1.5 metres to the middle and a mizzen mast. In this new configuration it was predicted the boat would be faster than *Fisher & Paykel*, although this did not prove to be the case for the 1992 Route of Discovery Race which *Publiespaña* (ex-*F&P*) won convincingly.

It is the third time that Tabacalera SA has sponsored a boat and for this race the crew will largely be drawn from veterans of previous campaigns. British skipper Lawrie Smith was a late signing. He brings with him a core of his old *Rothmans* crew.

WHITBREAD 60s

Boat: Intrum Justitia

Flag: Europe
Skipper: Roger Nilson
Designer: Bruce Farr
When Sweden's Roger Nilson asked Europe-wide debt collection company, Intrum Justitia, to sponsor his fourth Whitbread campaign, they agreed, on the condition that the twelve crew represented as many European nationals as possible. This in turn gave Nilson the opportunity to select the cream of the Continent's sailors. Dutch navigator, Marcel van Triest raced the 1989-90 Whitbread on *Equity & Law II*, but shot to prominence as one of the navigators in 1991's victorious French Admiral's Cup team. Other heavies include Swedish America's Cup skipper Gunnar Krantz and French Admiral's Cupper *Corum Saphir*'s skipper Pierre Mas.

Nilson also poached one of Fehlmann's 'afterguard' – Swiss sailor Dominique Wavre who was more recently coach to the French America's Cup team. Other nationalities include a Dane, a Finn, an Englishman and a German. Magnus Olsson, a veteran of two Whitbreads and an America's Cup, has co-ordinated the design and build of the boat.

It will be interesting to watch the concept of the EC being played out on a 60ft boat and how Nilson holds a group of such strong individuals together. By choosing a Farr design, he has voted with the majority, so ultimately the crew is his key to success.

Boat: Brooksfield

Flag: Italy
Skipper: Guido Maisto
Designer: Luc Bouvet & Olivier Petit
Guido Maisto was one of the first to secure sponsorship for this new class and he immediately commissioned a design from French naval architects Bouvet & Petit. As the designers of Titouan Lamazou's 1990 Globe Challenge-winner, *Ecureuil d'Aquitaine*, and the second-placed *Lada Poch*, they had the experience and track record in water-ballasted 60-footers that other designers lacked.

Brooksfield was built by Tencara, a high-tech shipyard near Venice that was set up specifically to build Raul Gardini's five America's Cup yachts. The boat was launched in October 1992, in time for the Route of Discovery Race from Spain to Miami. The race was billed as the first clash between the maxis and a W60, but it was a disappointment as the boat did not perform in the predominantly light weather. She arrived in Miami with keel problems and had to be shipped back to Italy for modifications.

This is Maisto's debut as a Whitbread skipper, although he was a watch leader on *Gatorade* in the 1989-90 race. *Gatorade* veterans Hervé Jan (navigator), Richard Brisius and Andrea Proto are key crew members.

Boat: Yamaha

Flag: Japan/New Zealand
Skipper: Ross Field
Designer: Bruce Farr
Yamaha has been the pace-setter for other Whitbread 60 campaigns. They were the first to announce full sponsorship and the first to launch. *Yamaha* was also the first syndicate in the history of the race to mount a two-boat campaign.

The first *Yamaha* was launched in April 1992 and raced extensively, covering 10,000 miles from New Zealand to Japan via Hawaii for the Kenwood Cup. Skipper Ross Field would not get specific about numbers, but there was always a tinge of excitement to his voice when he talked about the boat's performance and rumours of Whitbread 60s beating the maxis around the world soon flourished.

The second *Yamaha* was launched in April 1993. Notwithstanding his happiness with the first boat Ross Field had the hull shape, interior, deck layout and keel changed. With such a long time on the water with a confirmed crew, the *Yamaha* team has a significant advantage over other W60s.

Ross Field's crew are, like him, predominantly Whitbread veterans. He was a watch leader on *Steinlager 2* and has recruited fellow crew member Godfrey Cray. Other Whitbread veterans are Jeff Scott, Robbie Naismith and Steve Travurza. Joey Allen, Steve Cotton, Richard Bouzaid, Mark Hauser and Kazunori Komatsu from Japan complete the line-up.

Boat: Chuo Advertising

Flag: Japan/New Zealand
Skipper: Chris Dickson
Designer: Bruce Farr or John Swarbrick
The most novel approach to the Whitbread has been Chris Dickson's. Like *Yamaha* he chose a two-boat campaign, but with a twist. Two different designs were built simultaneously and then trialled to choose the faster. The first could be described as conventional – a Bruce Farr design similar to the other six Farr W60s. His second boat was definitely radical. Designed by little-known Western Australian designer John Swarbrick, the boat has a blunt nose, a wide stern and a radical keel which angles forward with a long torpedo bulb pointing back, forming a Z-shape. Swarbrick was one of the designers for the *Kookaburra*

America's Cup syndicate and the Japanese America's Cup boats.

This is Chris Dickson's first Whitbread having concentrated on America's Cup campaigns and winning world match racing championships (four times at the last count). This gives him a fresh approach to the Whitbread and he has called in other top international sailors who have yet to do a Whitbread – UK Olympic sailor Stuart Childerley, Australian Andrew Cape, American Mark Rudiger and Japanese Ken Hara. He does have Whitbread experience on board in Barry McKay and Matthew Smith.

Boat: Galicia 93

Flag: Spain
Skipper: Javier de la Gandara
Designer: Bruce Farr

Galicia, which stretches along the north-west coast of Spain, has a long sea-faring tradition. When the regional government decided to promote Galicia to the world and expatriate Galicians, a W60 seemed the natural choice. The Galician Sailing Federation is organising the campaign and has selected local hero Javier de la Gandara as skipper. De la Gandara skippered the maxi *Fortuna* for two legs in the 1989-90 Whitbread including the second leg where *Fortuna* set a noon-to-noon record of 398 miles and exceeded 400 miles on several occasions. His crew will all be from Galicia.

Boat: Hetman Sahaidachny

Flag: Ukraine
Skipper: Eugene Platon
Designer: Bruce Farr

Eugene Platon is a veteran of the first, and last, Soviet Whitbread entrant *Fazisi* which raced around the world just at a time when East-West relations were changing forever. On his return to the Ukraine Platon started work on his own project and in September 1991 he anticipated events by announcing that the *Hetman Sahaidachny* campaign would promote Ukraine on the world stage. 'Our round the world action is supposed to be the first step in the consolidation of Ukrainian progressive political movements and establishing the sovereignty of the Republic of Ukraine,' he stated. Once Ukraine's independence was established in Spring 1992, Platon could concentrate on his boat.

The Farr design was built in Kharkov at a former defence industry aviation plant using more advanced technology than is usually available in a boatyard. Lasers were used to line up the frames for the mould, leaving an error margin of only 0.02-0.03mm. By showing what Ukraine can do in the Whitbread, Platon hopes to attract more business for his low cost, high technology boat building.

His Ukrainian crew include *Fazisi* veterans Volodymyr Musatov and Yuri Doroshenko, Olympic yachtsman Yuri Tokovoi, Soviet Soling champion Sergei Pichugin, Yuri Semeniuk and Ivan Costiuchenko.

Boat: Odessa

Flag: Ukraine/USA
Skipper: Anatoly Verba
Designer: Igor Sidenko

This syndicate is also a product of the *Fazisi* campaign. It started out as a Soviet-American joint venture, then became a Russian/Ukrainian/American joint venture and finally a Ukrainian/American campaign.

The boat was designed by Igor Sidenko, who was a consultant to the abortive 1992 Red Star America's Cup campaign in San Diego. Construction of the yacht began in Russia at Volga Buran (builders of the first Soviet Space Shuttle) in June 1991 but *Odessa* was not handed over until October 1992 due to problems caused by the disintegration of the Soviet Union. She was then shipped in January 1993 to Tampa, Florida, for finishing.

Overcoming the problems of building a boat and organising a campaign were helped to some extent by the fact that *Odessa* had American partners working to raise money and support. It is likely that there will be American sailors on board but the core crew will be Ukrainian under skipper Anatoly Verba.

Boat: Winston

Flag: USA
Skipper: Dennis Conner and Brad Butterworth
Designer: Bruce Farr

Dennis Conner's announcement that he would be heading a campaign for the Whitbread surprised everyone, not least because he commissioned Bruce Farr to design the boat. The choice of Farr should not have been surprising, except that, during the acrimonious 1988 America's Cup, Conner described the designer of the Kiwi Big Boat as a 'loser' at an infamous press conference.

More used to working within the constraining nationality restrictions of the America's Cup, Conner appears to have relished the opportunity to mount a more international campaign. Firstly he appointed New Zealander Brad Butterworth to co-skipper the boat and select an international crew. Then, the Italian yard of CCYD near Venice was contracted to build *Winston*.

Conner is, perhaps, famous for being the man who lost and won back the America's Cup. He has won it on three other occasions and is well-known for his many championship wins in inshare racing. What is less well known is that he has won the SORC four times and has competed in a wide variety of off-shore events. As a watch leader on *Steinlager 2* Brad Butterworth has glowing Whitbread qualifications but he also has a track record in the America's Cup. The afterguard are Irishman Gordon Maguire, Italian Matteo Plazzi and Dutchman Bouwe Bekking. The rest of the crew are Frenchman Alexis Hellouin de Cenival and New Zealanders Dean Phipps, Peter Vitali, Dave Hurley, Mark Christianson and Matthew Mason.

Part Four

Results and Index

The Previous Races

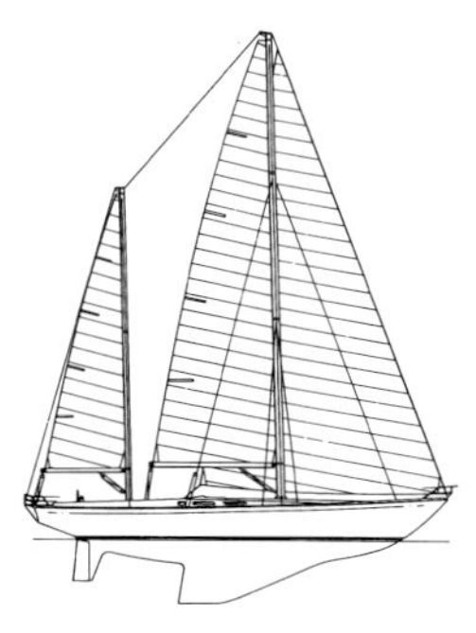

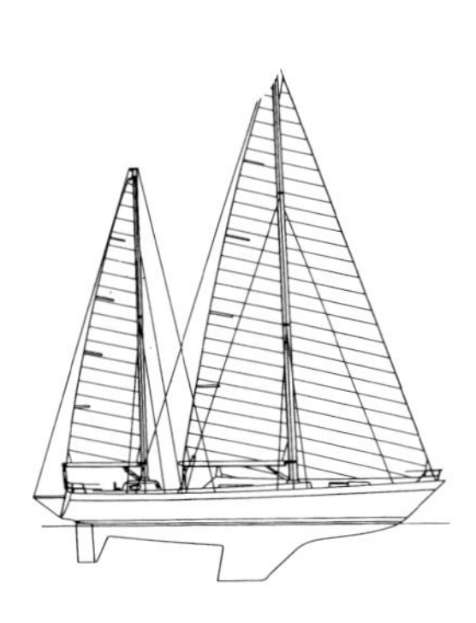

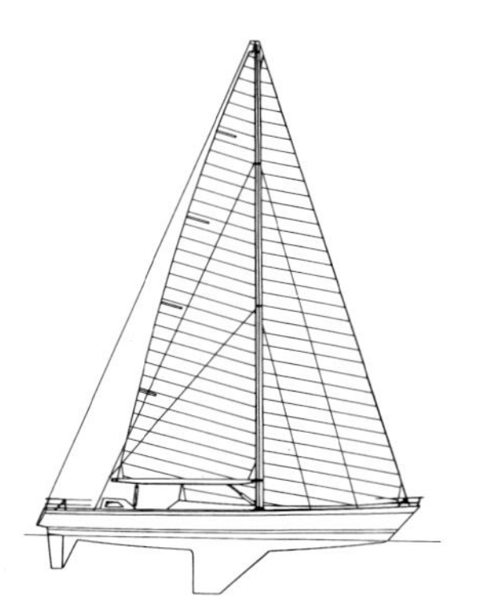

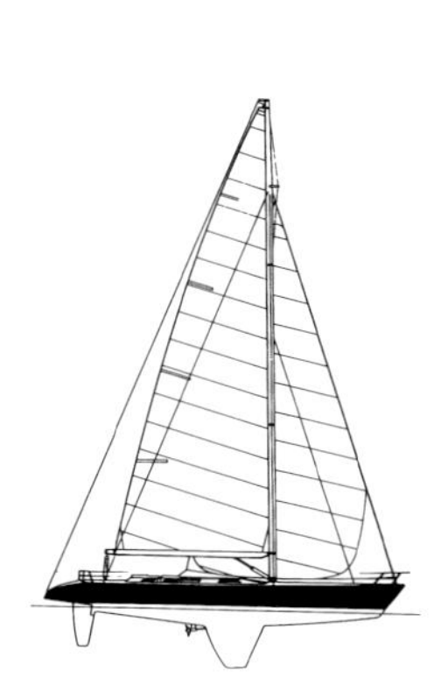

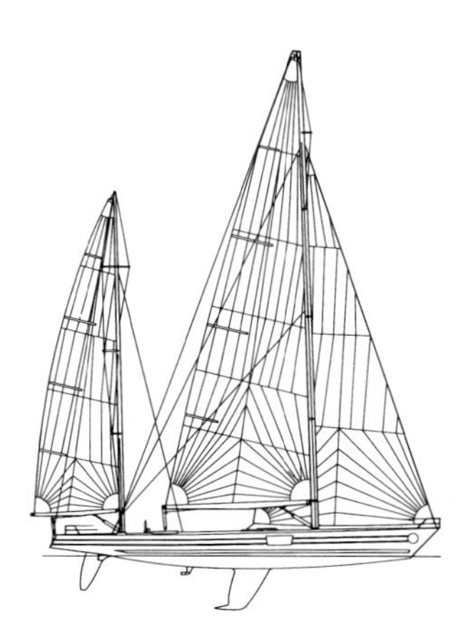

1973-74
Sayula II
Among the best sources of knowledge for serious ocean-going racers before the first Whitbread were the designers Olin and Rod Stephens who had been improving the breed, ever since 1933. The builder Nautor had an enviable reputation with Swans by the same designers.
Skipper
Ramon Carlin,
Mexico
Designer
Sparkman & Stephens,
USA
Builder
Nautor Swan,
Finland
LOA 65ft 19.8m
Beam 16.3ft 5.0m
Displ 56,370lb 25,590kg

1977-78
Flyer
Sparkman & Stephens developed this boat from *Sayula* to which she has a close resemblance in length, rig and visible profile. The beam was exactly the same; she weighed a little less in aluminium. The Dutch builder was one of the world's best at the time. The deck and interior were fashioned for round the world racing.
Skipper
Cornelis van Rietschoten,
The Netherlands
Designer
Sparkman & Stephens,
USA
Builder
Huisman-Vollenhove,
The Netherlands
LOA 65.1ft 19.8m
Beam 16.3ft 5.0m
Displ 55,000lb 25,000kg

1981-82
Flyer
The designer served his time at the famous S&S and has been a leading favourite for ocean racing yachts for virtually the whole era of the Whitbread. The purpose of the design was to finish first on every leg, although in the end, she won the race overall.
Skipper
Cornelis van Rietschoten,
The Netherlands
Designer
German Frers,
Argentina
Builder
Huisman-Vollenhove,
The Netherlands
LOA 76.0ft 23.2m
Beam 18.0ft 5.5m
Displ 67,000lb 30,390kg

1985-86
L'Esprit d'Equipe
The story can be read of how major damage prevented this boat completing the 1981-82 race and how she was refitted and turned into a winner. With a light hull and fractional rig, she was able to carry a relatively small crew, who in turn needed less food and water.
Skipper
Lionel Péan,
France
Designer
Philippe Briand,
France
Builder
Labb and Richeux/
Dufour,
France
LOA 57.7ft 17.6m
Beam 15.8ft 4.8m
Displ 32,930lb 14,935kg

1989-90
Steinlager 2
At least up to early 1993, this was the ultimate Whitbread racer. Bruce Farr's design office is currently one of the busiest in the world in the creation of ocean racing boats. In this design, length and sail area were carried to their maximum under the rule.
Skipper
Peter Blake,
New Zealand
Designer
Bruce Farr,
NZ/USA
Builder
Southern Pacific,
New Zealand
LOA 84ft 25.6m
Beam 19.2ft 5.85m
Displ 68,000lb, 30,845kg

1973-74	**Leg 1**			**Leg 2**			**Leg 3**			**Leg 4**			**Overall Results**		
Boat/days.hrs	elapsed	corrected	place	elapsed	corrected	place	elapsed	corrected	place	elapsed	corrected	place	elapsed	corrected	place
Sayula II	44.05	39.14	2	30.14	26.00	1	42.14	36.18	2	35.00	31.04	4	152.09	133.13	1
Adventure	43.02	36.09	1	39.06	32.13	9	45.01	36.13	1	35.10	29.12	1	162.19	135.08	2
Grand Louis	48.07	42.13	9	31.22	26.13	2	45.14	38.09	4	36.06	31.12	5	162.01	138.15	3
Kriter	46.09	42.13	8	30.13	26.18	3	42.16	37.21	3	37.00	33.21	8	156.14	141.02	4
Guia	49.07	40.17	5	38.06	29.18	7	51.06	40.11	5	39.00	31.22	6	177.19	142.19	5
Great Britain II	43.05	43.05	12	29.17	29.17	6	40.16	40.16	6	30.21	30.21	2	144.11	144.11	6
Second Life	45.17	43.02	11	30.09	27.18	4	45.18	42.10	8	39.06	37.02	11	161.02	150.08	7
CSeRB	51.06	43.12	13	39.09	31.16	8	51.17	41.22	7	44.16	38.05	13	187.00	155.07	8
British Soldier	49.04	43.13	14	40.07	34.17	10	49.17	42.15	9	40.16	36.00	10	179.20	156.21	9
Tauranga	49.00	41.22	7	43.17	36.16	12	52.02	43.03	10	41.02	35.05	9	185.21	156.22	10
Copernicus	51.16	42.08	8	45.21	36.15	11	57.13	45.19	12	49.18	42.01	14	204.20	166.19	11
33 Export	45.07	39.19	3	57.19	52.08	16	58.15	51.16	14	35.17	31.04	3	197.10	174.22	12
Otago	52.03	45.12	15	44.11	38.07	13	58.13	50.16	13	48.17	43.13	15	203.21	178.09	13
Peter von Danzig	52.12	46.09	16	44.15	38.13	14	53.00	45.07	11	54.12	49.11	16	204.16	179.15	14
Pen Duick VI	57.09	57.00	17	29.08	28.01	5	–	–	–	–	–	–	–	–	–
Burton Cutter	42.00	41.04	6	–	–	–	–	–	–	33.00	31.11	7	–	–	–
Jakaranda	46.08	40.07	4	–	–	–	–	–	–	–	–	–	–	–	–
Concorde	–	–	–	50.02	40.20	15	–	–	–	–	–	–	–	–	–
Pen Duick III	–	–	–	–	–	–	–	–	–	42.15	37.18	12	–	–	–

1977–78 Boat/days.hrs.min.sec	Leg 1 elapsed	corrected	place	Leg 2 elapsed	corrected	place	Leg 3 elapsed	corrected	place	Leg 4 elapsed	corrected	place	Overall Results elapsed	corrected	place
Flyer	38.20.54.00	34.13.52.12	1	32.05.02.24	27.12.15.00	4	34.05.23.24	29.12.34.48	2	30.22.08.24	27.10.18.00	7	136.05.28.48	119.01.00.36	1
King's Legend	38.22.54.00	34.15.52.12	2	32.03.50.24	27.11.01.48	3	36.16.12.00	31.23.23.24	7	30.20.51.00	27.09.00.00	5	138.15.47.24	121.11.17.24	2
Traité de Rome	45.11.57.00	37.06.45.00	5	36.12.01.48	27.10.25.48	2	39.15.13.48	30.13.38.24	3	33.05.45.00	26.12.01.48	2	154.20.58.12	121.18.51.00	3
Disque d'Or	41.07.45.00	36.10.36.36	4	33.09.10.48	28.00.40.12	5	36.16.22.12	31.07.51.36	4	30.15.19.48	26.00.39.31	3	142.00.37.48	122.10.56.24	4
ADC Accutrac	43.04.53.24	38.12.19.12	9	34.06.36.36	29.03.10.48	7	36.23.00.00	31.19.34.48	5	31.04.58.12	27.09.13.48	6	145.15.28.12	126.20.18.36	5
Gauloises II	43.03.18.36	35.18.35.24	3	44.12.42.36	36.09.54.00	15	37.08.24.00	29.05.35.24	1	31.22.36.00	25.21.49.12	1	156.23.00.36	127.07.54.36	6
Adventure	45.00.52.12	37.11.10.12	6	36.11.39.00	28.03.18.00	6	42.19.35.24	34.11.14.24	14	34.06.06.36	28.01.12.36	8	158.14.12.36	128.02.55.12	7
Neptune	43.19.55.12	38.09.56.24	8	38.01.55.48	32.03.08.24	10	37.19.05.24	31.20.18.00	6	32.12.37.12	28.02.29.24	9	152.05.33.36	130.11.52.48	8
B&B Italia	44.05.28.12	37.23.23.24	7	39.08.11.24	32.11.03.00	12	39.09.45.00	32.12.34.48	9	34.06.10.12	29.03.24.00	12	157.05.34.48	132.02.22.48	9
33 Export	50.06.12.36	43.10.21.00	13	34.14.55.12	27.02.25.12	1	43.05.04.48	35.16.34.48 c	15	32.09.19.12	26.19.09.36	4	164.15.31.48	133.00.31.12	10
Tielsa	42.22.00.00	39.00.45.00	10	37.13.31.12	33.07.36.36	14	36.17.27.00	32.11.33.00	8	31.08.25.12	28.04.41.24	10	148.13.22.12	133.00.36.00	11
Great Britain II	40.05.36.00	40.03.57.00	12	31.06.34.12	31.06.34.12	9	33.16.46.12	33.16.46.12 b	10	29.07.25.48	29.07.25.48	13	134.12.22.48	134.10.43.12	12
Debenhams	45.09.06.00	39.01.30.36	11	39.08.12.00	32.09.21.36	11	41.03.17.24	34.04.27.00	12	35.08.30.36	30.04.30.36	15	161.05.05.24	135.19.49.48	13
Japy-Hermes	51.13.42.36	46.09.12.36	14	38.08.37.48	32.15.55.48	13	39.21.48.00	34.05.06.36 d	13	34.05.20.24	29.23.44.24	14	164.01.29.24	143.06.00.00	14
Heath's Condor	50.07.28.48	51.00.54.00 a	15	30.09.03.36	30.10.54.00	8	33.17.10.12	33.19.00.36	11	28.15.59.24	28.07.13.12	11	143.01.42.00	144.00.00.21	15

1981–82 Boat/days.hrs.min.sec	Leg 1 elapsed	corrected	place	Leg 2 elapsed	corrected	place	Leg 3 elapsed	corrected	place	Leg 4 elapsed	corrected	place	Overall Results elapsed	corrected	place
Flyer	36.10.56.37	36.03.06.57	3	30.04.27.30	29.20.31.44	3	24.01.22.20	23.18.38.19	8	29.13.47.47	29.06.55.48	2	120.06.34.14	119.01.12.48	1
Charles Heidsieck III	38.14.37.20	35.12.35.20	2	32.20.45.55	29.17.46.15	2	25.17.44.47	23.02.03.46	5	34.16.26.33	31.23.30.08	4	131.21.34.35	120.07.55.29	2
Kriter IX	38.17.22.45	35.00.38.39	1	33.15.58.22	29.22.05.09	4	27.01.24.42	23.21.04.55	9	34.20.51.53	31.15.01.43	3	134.07.37.42	120.10.50.26	3
Disque d'Or 3	43.05.25.00	37.21.05.41	7	35.19.18.56	30.09.19.40	6	26.18.09.43	22.03.46.46	2	37.18.06.49 h	33.01.33.10	10	143.13.00.28	123.11.45.17	4
Outward Bound	45.00.03.27	37.18.21.55	6	38.23.28.51	31.15.32.02	11	28.22.51.35	22.17.26.59	4	38.16.55.37	32.08.34.07	7	151.15.19.30	124.11.55.03	5(1)
Xargo III	44.20.33.21	38.17.20.52	10	36.18.54.19	30.15.26.51	7	27.14.48.52	22.10.17.31	3	38.08.53.46	32.23.57.23	8	147.15.10.18	124.19.02.37	6
Mor bihan	46.21.35.22	38.15.57.57	9	39.22.39.53	31.14.28.33	10	29.01.56.02	21.23.56.17	1	40.14.23.00	33.09.01.58	13	156.12.34.17	125.15.24.45	7(2)
Berge Viking	43.22.05.46	37.11.25.42	4	37.17.02.30	31.04.21.58	8	29.13.20.06	24.00.17.23	10	38.16.29.29	33.00.49.14	9	149.20.57.51	125.16.54.17	8
Alaska Eagle	41.21.19.03	37.16.18.49	5	36.12.24.22	32.06.22.30	13	27.22.22.42	24.07.53.02	12	35.20.50.45	32.04.17.23	5	142.14.56.52	126.10.51.44	9
Euromarché	42.02.40.30	40.00.09.45	20	32.04.45.47	30.04.06.19	5	25.09.24.50	23.16.33.46	7	34.22.37.35	33.02.47.50	11	134.15.28.42	126.23.37.40	10
Ceramco New Zealand	47.07.28.05	46.01.00.49	26	30.12.51.14	29.06.00.14	1	24.08.39.24	23.06.27.35	6	30.06.56.55	29.04.14.05	1	132.11.55.38	127.17.42.43	11
Skopbank of Finland	47.11.29.54	39.12.54.15	18	39.08.23.21	31.07.19.15	9	31.01.32.35	24.05.35.39	11	40.12.28.42	33.13.17.38	14	158.09.54.32	128.15.06.47	12 (3)
RollyGo	48.02.31.56	40.17.31.47	21	39.20.17.41	32.08.59.40	14	30.18.30.32	24.10.15.05	13	38.19.21.24	32.08.05.40	6	157.12.41.33	129.20.52.12	13 (4)
Traité de Rome	48.10.45.15	38.23.20.21	12	42.16.46.14	33.03.19.18	15	33.17.40.07	25.15.11.22	14	41.13.28.33	33.06.07.40	12	166.10.40.09	130.23.58.41	14 (5)
Croky	48.14.29.19	38.23.53.55	13	43.06.25.20	33.12.50.20	17	34.23.54.41	26.17.33.28	15	43.03.33.04	34.17.17.00	15	170.00.22.44	133.23.34.43	15 (6)
FCF Challenger	39.08.48.35 f	39.08.48.35	15	33.18.15.32 f	33.18.15.32	18	27.04.37.03	27.04.37.03	16	38.07.46.02	38.07.46.02	20	138.15.27.12	138.15.27.12	16
United Friendly	44.22.46.07	44.05.07.05	25	35.20.03.14	35.04.30.05	20	27.19.45.51	27.07.10.59	17	35.07.48.38	34.17.18.46	16	143.22.23.50	141.10.06.55	17
Walross III Berlin	48.09.34.05	39.10.53.50	17	45.22.49.35	36.22.24.08	21	37.04.56.03 g	29.13.45.43	18	45.17.57.01	37.20.32.22	19	177.07.16.44	143.19.36.03	18 (7)
Licor 43	45.23.20.42	42.02.21.55	22	52.13.31.53	48.15.20.40	24	37.10.46.39	34.02.47.46	20	38.15.19.48	35.05.46.14	17	174.14.59.02	160.02.16.35	19
Ilgagomma	50.06.34.10 e	43.00.52.38	24	46.17.29.19	39.09.32.30	23	36.21.28.42 f	30.16.04.06	19	53.15.15.11	47.06.53.41	23	187.12.47.22	160.09.22.55	20 (8)
Bubblegum	48.04.21.36 e	38.06.42.05	8	43.08.15.44	33.07.31.07	16	Retired	–	–	46.00.24.47	37.07.56.42	18	–	–	–
European Uni Belgium	48.06.42.56	38.17.24.31	11	Retired	–	–	53.17.29.50	45.10.29.27	21	47.16.36.34	39.06.41.52	21	–	–	–
Gauloises 3	43.15.36.30	39.19.51.19	19	35.22.11.20	32.01.14.41	12	Retired	–	–	DNS	–	–	–	–	–
Save Venice	46.01.14.16	43.00.20.02	23	40.13.02.53	37.11.11.52	22	DNS	–	–	DNS	–	–	–	–	–
Swedish Entry	44.00.58.30	39.06.17.01	14	39.17.23.21	34.21.12.32	19	DNS	–	–	DNS	–	–	–	–	–
Vivanapoli	71.09.37.41 e	64.20.39.45	27	DNS	–	–	DNS	–	–	60.07.09.45	54.13.28.34	24	–	–	–
33 Export	44.22.15.56	39.10.26.19	16	Retired	–	–	DNS	–	–	DNS	–	–	–	–	–
La Barca Laboratorio	Retired	–	–	DNS	–	–	DNS	–	–	47.07.00.01	44.02.13.23	22	–	–	–
Scandanavian	Retired	–	–	DNS	–	–	DNS	–	–	DNS	–	–	–	–	–

1985–86 Boat/days.hrs.min.sec	Leg 1 elapsed	corrected	place	Leg 2 elapsed	corrected	place	Leg 3 elapsed	corrected	place	Leg 4 elapsed	corrected	place	Overall Results elapsed	corrected	place
L'Esprit d'Equipe	37.13.41.25	32.07.07.47	1	34.01.59.01	28.17.46.50	2	27.00.50.39	22.07.54.53	1	33.07.44.14	28.14.20.19	1	132.00.15.19	111.23.09.49	1
Philips Innovator	36.12.28.11	32.18.38.09	2	31.12.57.26	27.17.57.26	1	26.09.19.51	23.01.10.20	4	32.16.15.12	29.07.45.42	2	127.03.00.40	112.21.31.37	2
Fazer Finland	36.10.33.09	32.23.15.55	3	32.17.45.45	29.05.23.40	8	26.12.15.43	23.09.56.43	5	32.12.50.24	29.10.12.52	3	128.05.25.01	115.00.49.10	3
UBS	34.01.39.20	33.23.05.31	4	29.04.59.22	29.02.23.34	6	24.14.11.20	24.11.54.06	7	29.17.41.40	29.15.23.51	4	117.14.31.42	117.04.47.03	4
Rucanor Tristar	42.01.40.04	36.12.49.49 a	10	34.14.23.10	28.23.49.28	5	27.21.05.10	22.22.33.21	3	34.21.17.57	29.22.16.34	5	139.10.26.21	118.09.29.12	5
Fortuna Lights	38.18.46.48	34.08.09.55	5	35.12.04.53	31.00.04.59	12	28.05.18.15	24.06.10.21	6	35.09.12.00	31.09.41.22	8	137.21.22.56	121.00.06.37	6
Lion New Zealand	34.17.46.47	34.11.45.25	6	29.18.58.12	29.12.52.08	10	25.22.53.59	25.17.31.32	11	31.18.52.00	31.13.29.13	10	122.06.31.58	121.07.38.18	7
Drum	36.16.44.23	36.13.44.48	11	29.13.31.04	29.10.02.59	9	24.23.30.35	24.20.27.17	8	31.13.08.29	31.10.04.25	8	122.18.54.31	122.06.19.29	8
Equity & Law	47.18.23.05	41.20.13.22	13	34.18.29.03	28.18.28.36	3	28.00.33.50	22.17.42.47	2	35.05.41.40	29.22.18.59	6	145.19.07.38	123.06.43.44	9
Côte d'Or	34.23.28.26	34.14.49.27	7	30.20.07.06	30.18.23.25	11	25.01.09.11	24.23.37.51	10	31.09.46.12	31.08.14.29	7	126.08.27.33	125.19.01.50	10
Shadow of Switzerland	43.06.12.14	36.09.16.08	9	41.13.35.24	34.14.30.25	13	31.21.08.43	25.17.58.04	12	37.21.58.03	31.18.10.42	11	154.14.54.50	128.11.55.19	11
Norsk Data GB	39.15.09.53	39.02.31.20	12	35.00.02.49	35.11.14.26	14	27.15.45.41	27.04.28.50	14	34.18.17.13	34.06.57.34	13	138.01.15.36	136.01.12.10	12
SAS Baia Viking	51.18.15.56	44.22.06.47	14	44.17.37.48	37.19.20.48	15	32.14.10.39	26.11.42.17	13	41.16.49.06	35.13.44.13	14	170.18.53.29	144.18.54.05	13
Atlantic Privateer	DNF	–	–	29.03.09.36	28.22.44.02	4	25.00.50.25	24.21.00.54	9	32.01.55.49	31.22.05.20	12	–	–	–
NZI Enterprise	35.09.06.42	35.09.06.42	8	29.03.11.56	29.03.11.56	7									

1989–90 Boat/days.hrs.min.sec	Leg 1 Elapsed time	place	Leg 2 Elapsed time	place	Leg 3 Elapsed time	place	Leg 4 Elapsed time	place	Leg 5 Elapsed time	place	Leg 6 Elapsed time	place	Overall result Elapsed time	place
DIVISION A														
Steinlager 2	25.20.46.27	1	27.05.34.44	1	12.17.33.00	1	22.20.41.53	1	22.16.41.11	1	17.00.23.15	1	128.09.40.30	1
Fisher & Paykel NZ	27.03.50.26	3	27.08.30.20	4	12.17.39.04	2	22.21.03.11	2	22.17.15.41	2	17.00.59.40	2	129.21.18.22	2
Merit	26.08.11.20	2	27.07.07.56	3	12.18.44.17	3	23.10.30.32 j	4	23.10.52.24	4	17.02.43.45	3	130.10.10.14 j	3
Rothmans	27.07.29.00	4	27.07.07.28	2	12.18.54.37	4	23.09.00.11	3	22.21.33.04	3	17.12.50.03	4	131.04.54.23	4
The Card	28.06.43.25	5	27.22.57.57	6	12.20.49.50	5	24.18.12.47	8	23.15.24.19	5	17.19.07.25	5	135.07.15.43	5
Charles Jourdan	28.20.10.18	11	27.22.16.41	5	13.02.53.49	9	23.14.18.05 j	5	24.11.34.24	12	18.16.01.34	13	136.15.14.51 j	6
Fortuna Extra Lights	28.19.49.45	10	28.05.52.22	9	12.21.22.22	6	25.01.17.31	11	24.10.07.05	11	17.21.44.56	7	137.08.14.11	7
Gatorade	28.13.22.58	7	29.05.39.14 a	11	13.05.11.08	11	24.17.28.29	7	24.05.03.34	10	18.15.44.49	12	138.14.30.12 a	8
Union Bank of Finland	29.13.49.05	14	28.05.13.52	8	14.20.40.06	16	23.18.12.29 j	6	24.00.33.43	7	18.06.08.57	9	138.16.38.12 j	9
Belmont Finland II	28.20.21.15	12	29.15.57.55	14	13.14.27.42	13	25.00.45.54	10	24.04.23.00	9	17.20.35.27	6	139.04.31.13	10
Fazisi	28.13.20.18	6	29.01.40.15	10	13.04.40.30	10	25.07.01.15	13	25.01.57.37	13	18.04.21.09	8	139.09.01.04	11
NCB Ireland	29.05.27.46	13	29.10.39.02	13	13.10.50.24	12	24.23.31.22	9	24.03.24.54	8	18.13.29.10	11	139.19.22.38	12
British Satquote Defender	28.14.23.52	9	29.10.01.43	12	12.23.29.25	8	25.01.31.12	12	23.18.49.47	6	23.16.26.24	21	143.12.42.23	13
Liverpool Enterprise	32.03.15.55	16	33.03.08.26	16	14.14.17.58	14	26.02.56.09	14	26.01.36.30	16	19.03.45.24	14	151.04.52.22	15
Martela OF	28.13.54.58	8	28.01.27.57	7	12.22.42.57	7	withdrew	–	–	–	–	–	–	–
DIVISION C (Open position is in brackets)														
Equity & Law II	31.09.57.53	1 (15)	31.22.28.36	1 (15)	14.16.55.13	1 (15)	26.15.34.24	1 (15)	25.20.45.39	1 (14)	18.10.08.48	1 (10)	148.23.50.33	1 (14)
DIVISION D														
Esprit de Liberté	34.09.02.59	1 (18)	36.18.09.59	4 (20)	15.06.17.16	2 (20)	29.03.25.51	1 (17)	27.02.41.10	1 (17)	22.05.59.01	2 (17)	164.21.36.16	1 (17)
Maiden	35.00.46.44	3 (20)	35.11.11.41	1 (17)	15.05.27.14	1 (19)	30.12.06.48	3 (20)	28.03.35.18	4 (21)	22.17.59.08	4 (19)	167.03.06.53	2 (18)
Schlussel von Bremen	35.11.46.37 a	4 (22)	36.18.06.42	3 (19)	15.08.21.58	3 (21)	29.20.33.28	2 (18)	28.02.43.03	3 (20)	22.05.35.46	1 (16)	167.19.07.34 a	3 (19)
La Poste	37.20.04.18	5 (23)	40.15.33.31	5 (23)	18.23.18.23	5 (23)	30.15.21.39	4 (21)	30.20.57.38	5 (22)	22.23.40.48	5 (20)	181.22.56.17	4 (21)
Rucanor Sport	34.10.20.03	2 (19)	36.17.57.43	2 (18)	15.23.31.41	4 (22)	withdrew	–	27.06.14.10	2 (18)	22.17.45.56	3 (18)	–	–
CRUISING DIVISION														
Creightons Naturally	34.07.59.15	1 (17)	40.09.45.43	2 (22)	15.04.12.04	2 (18)	26.16.10.48	1 (16)	25.21.22.18	1 (15)	19.19.04.50	1 (15)	162.06.34.58	1 (16)
With Integrity	35.07.11.47	2 (21)	37.18.19.55	1 (21)	14.22.50.02	1 (17)	29.21.14.03	2 (19)	28.01.17.10	2 (19)	24.17.26.10	2 (22)	170.16.19.07	2 (20)

a *Includes penalty* b *Includes 10 minute penalty* c *Includes 5 minute penalty* d *Includes 2 hour* allowance for assisting *33 Export* e *Half standard time penalty* f *Quarter standard time penalty*
g *10 Hours 29 minutes deducted for standing by Bubblegum* h *20 minute time penalty* i *Time amended by 30 minutes for damage at start* j *Time amended for assisting Martelo OF*

Index of People and Yachts